COLORING THE CRESCENT CITY

BY: VICTORIA ZEMKE

Copyright © 2020 Victoria Zemke
All rights reserved.
No part of this book may be reproduced
or distributed in any form.

For more products or info visit
www.homesweetnola.com

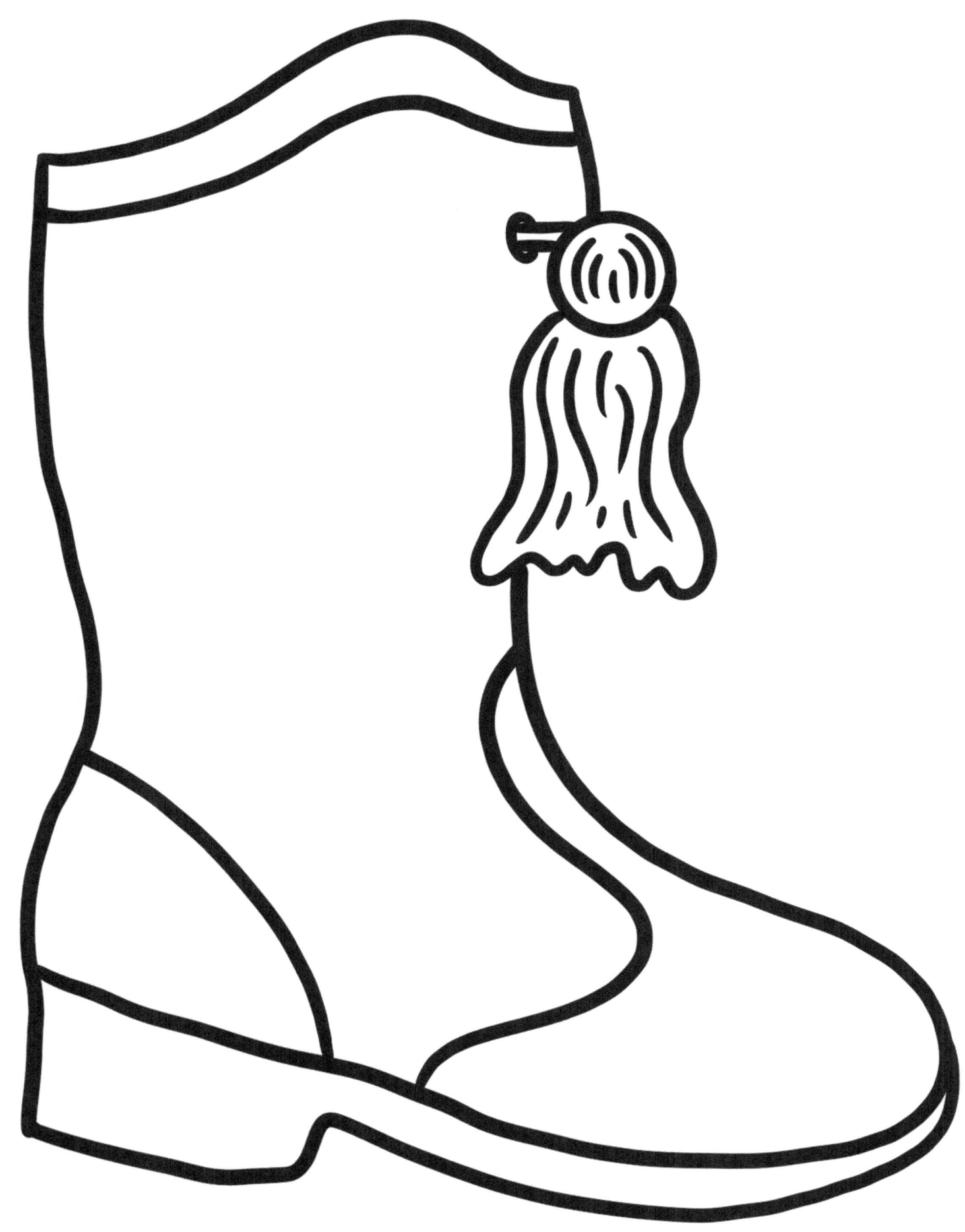

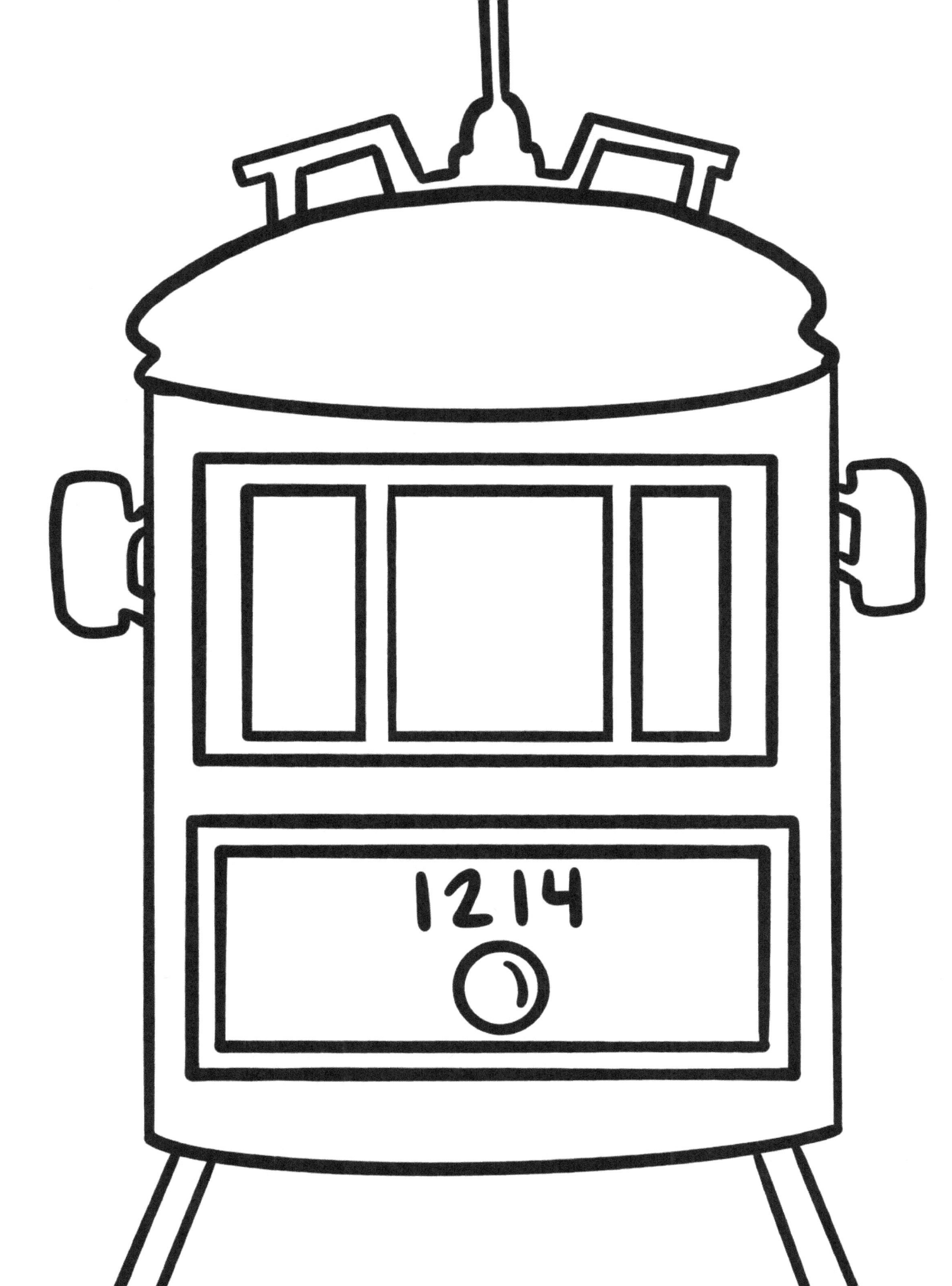

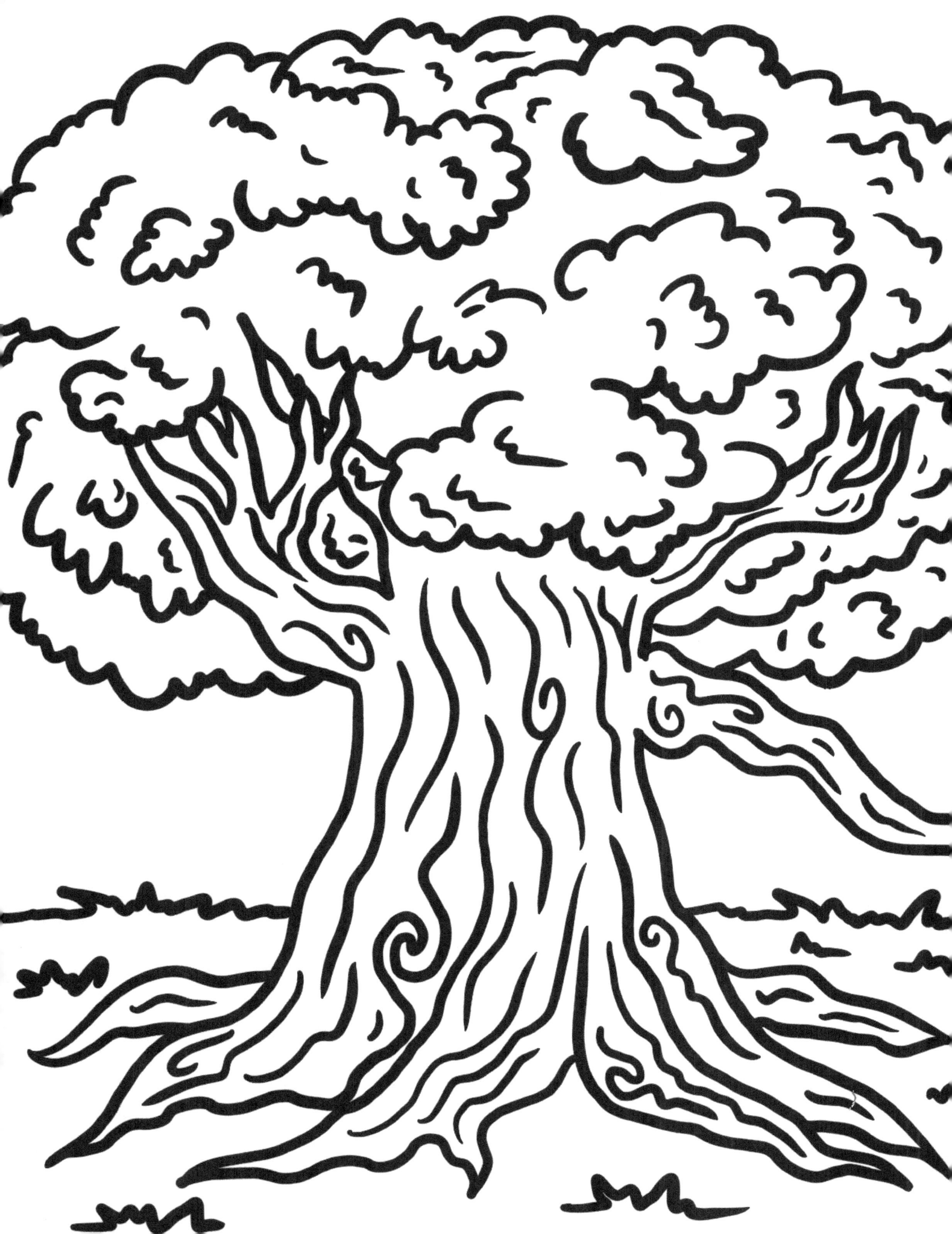

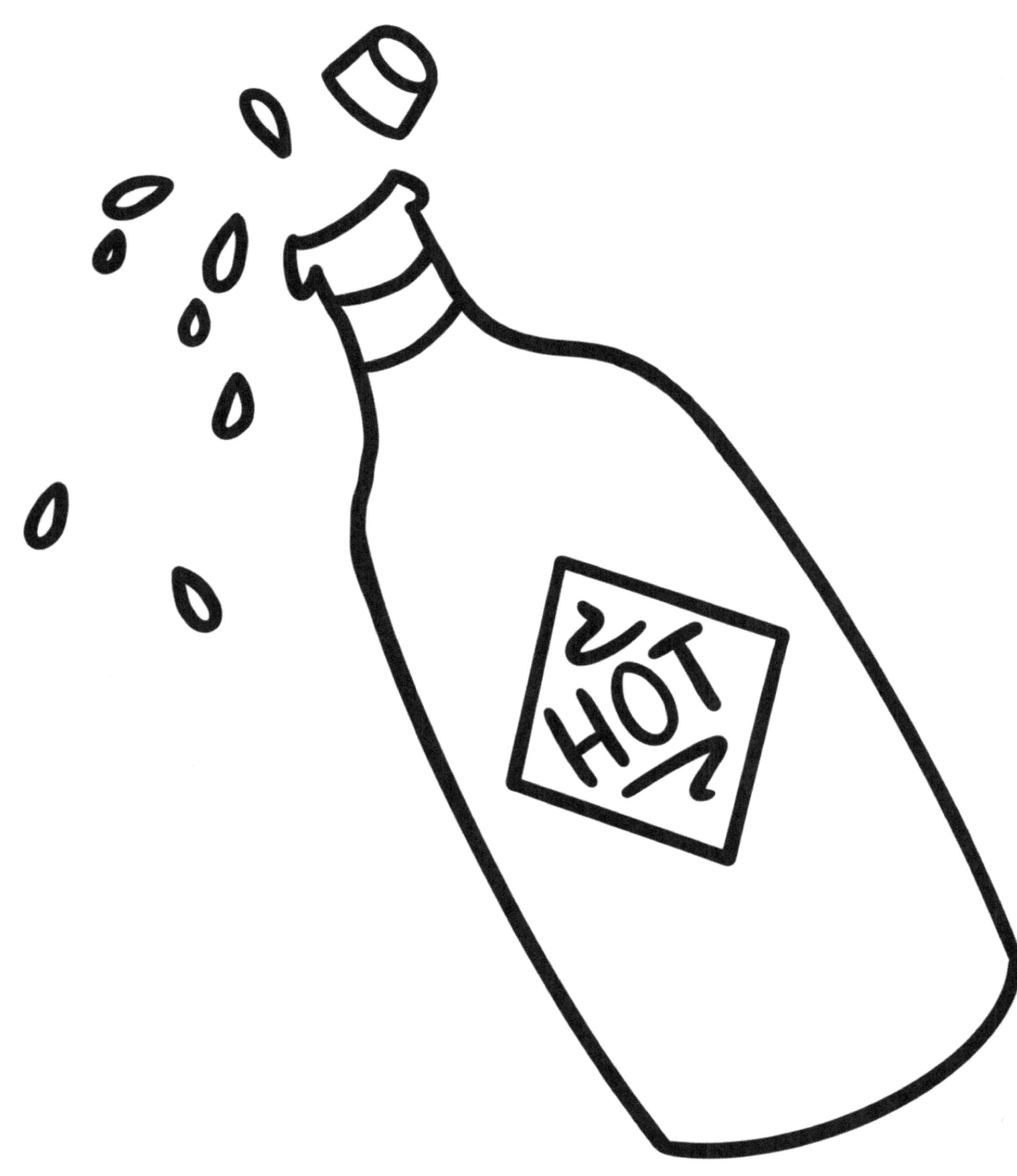

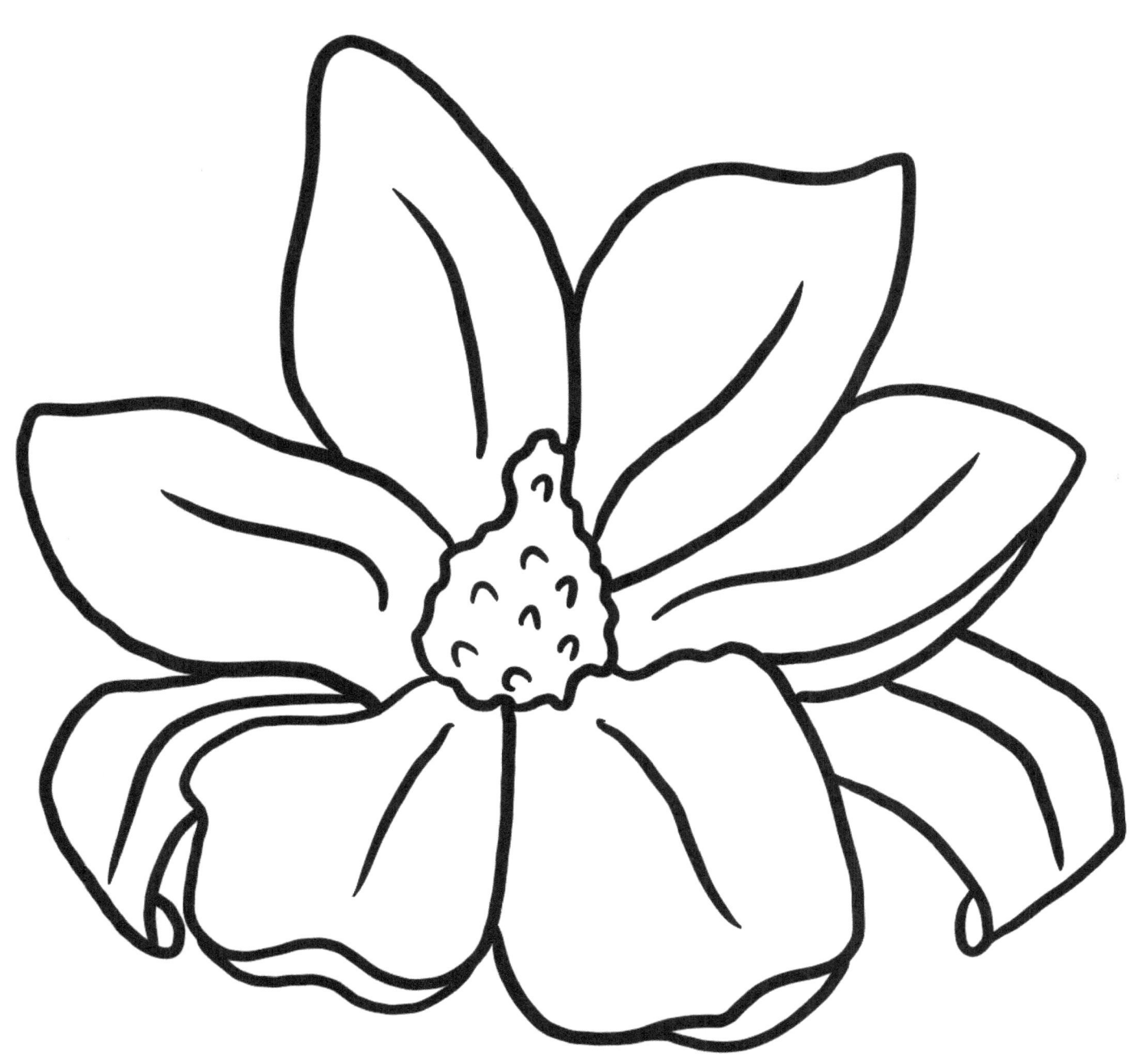

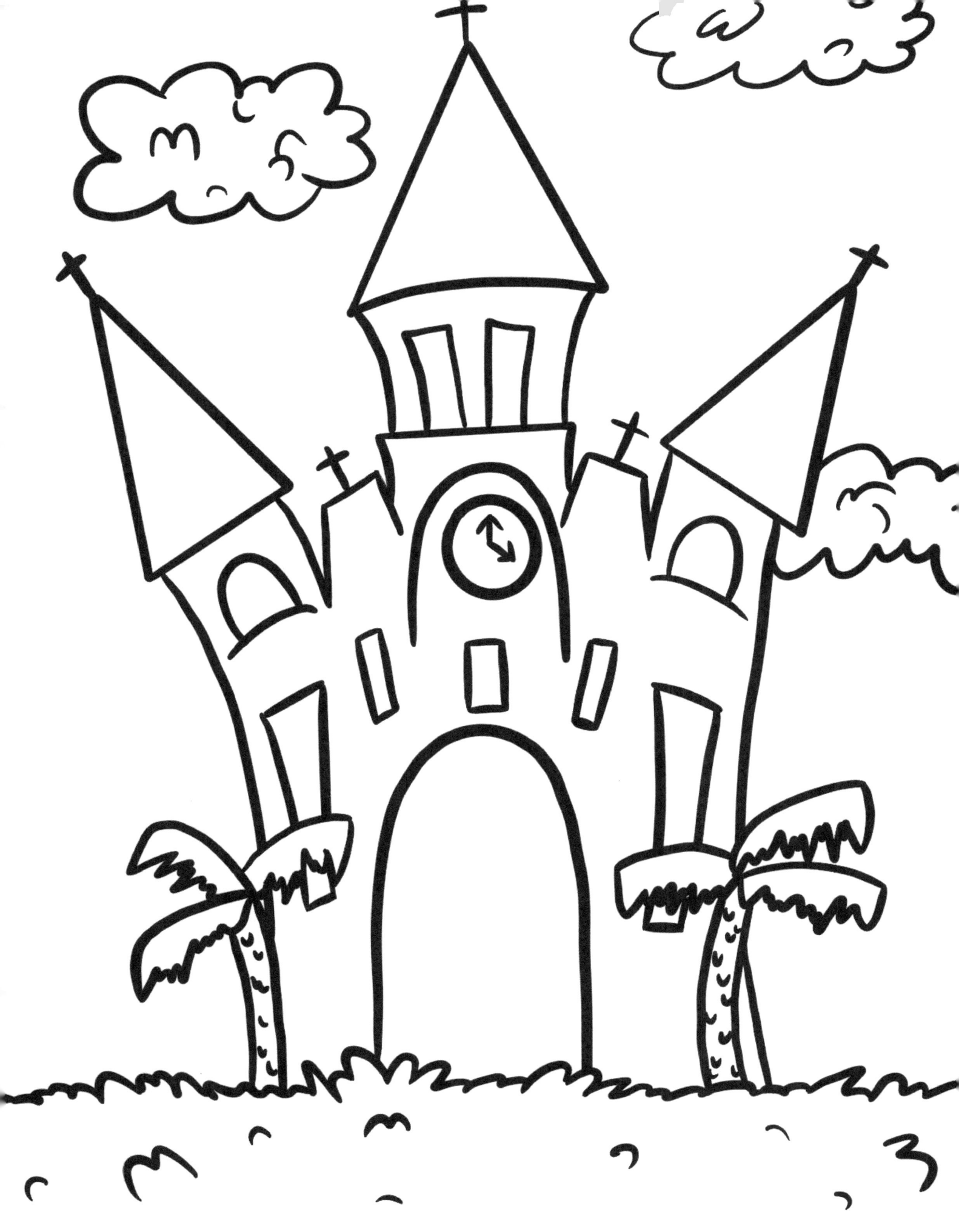

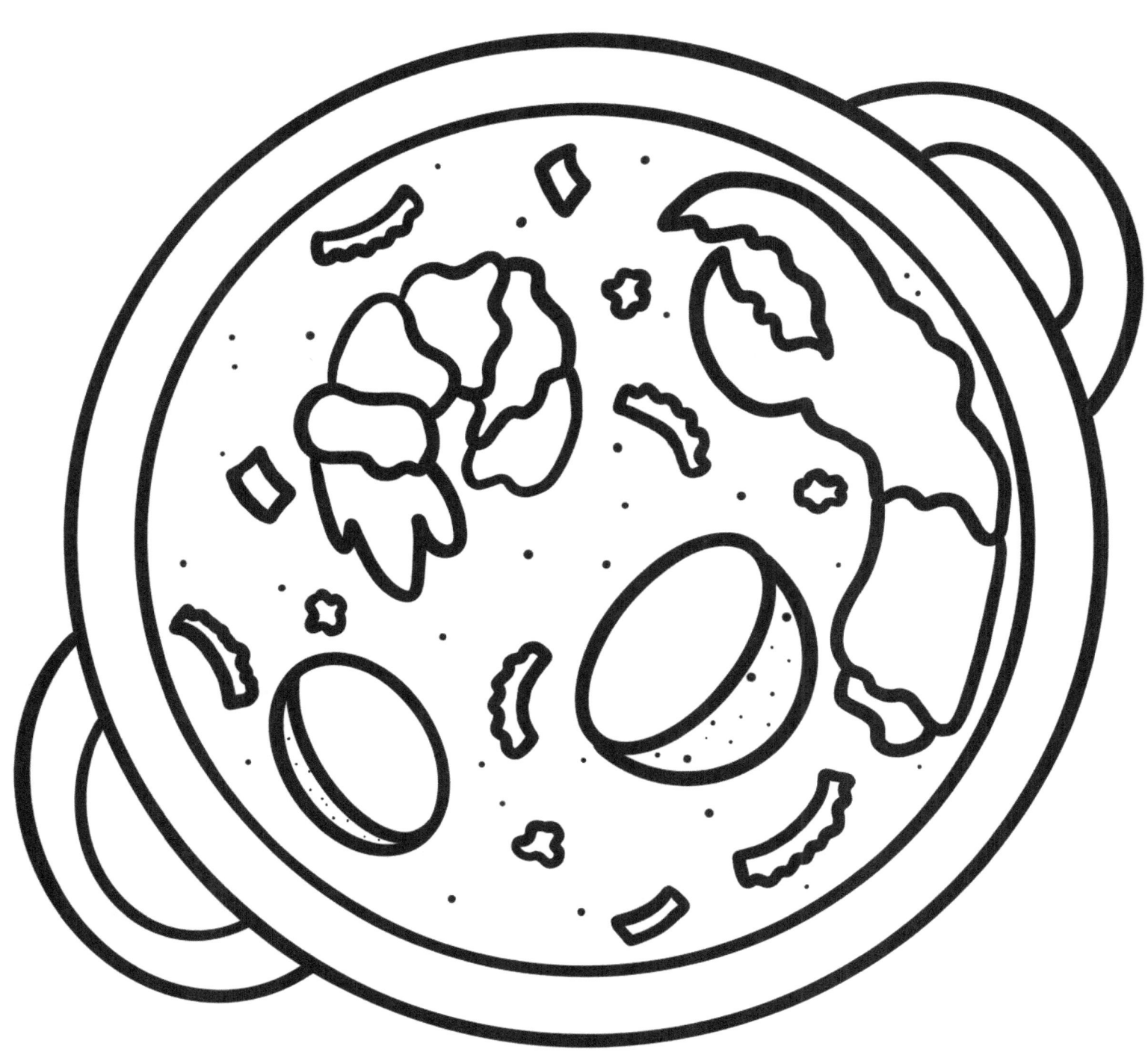

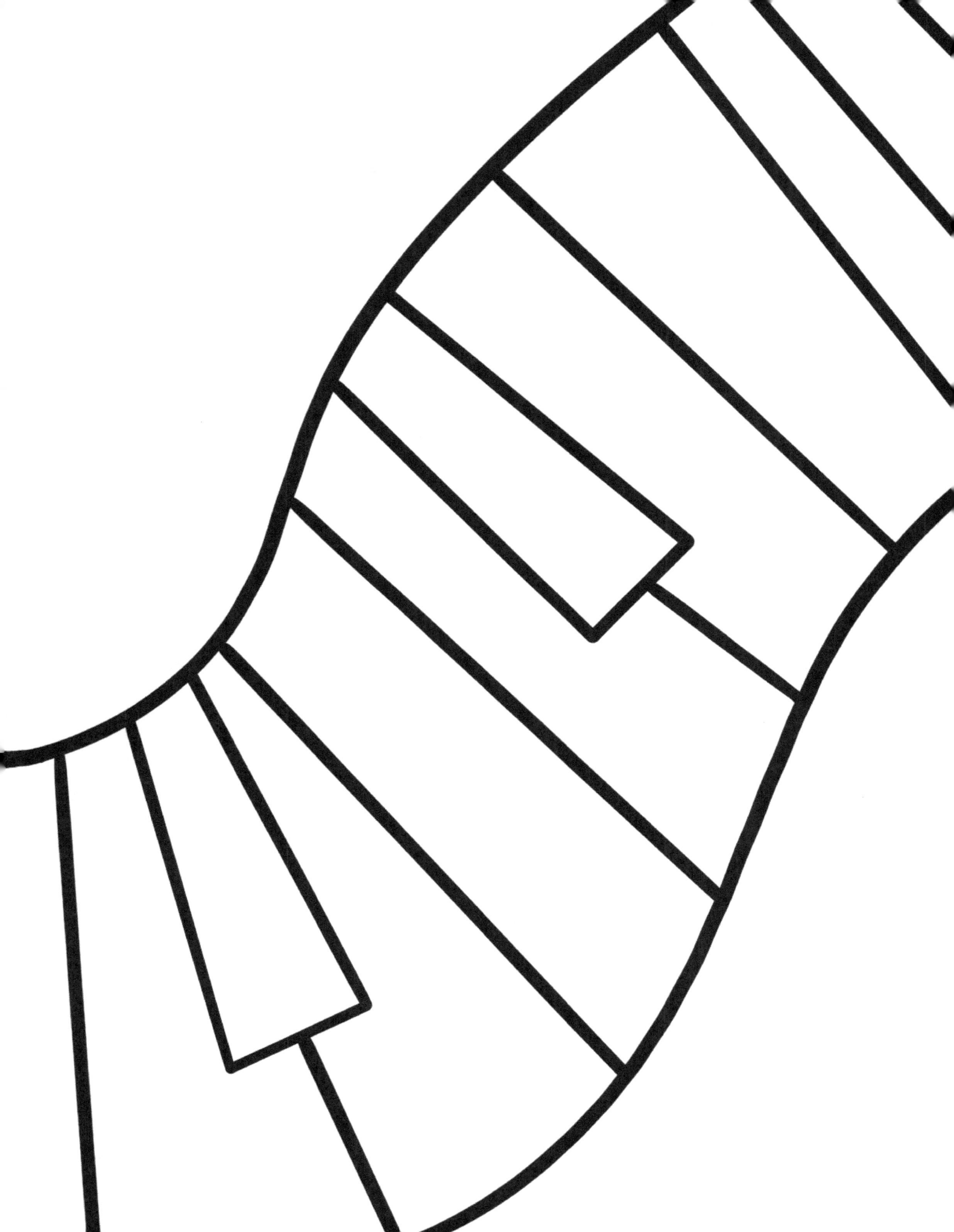

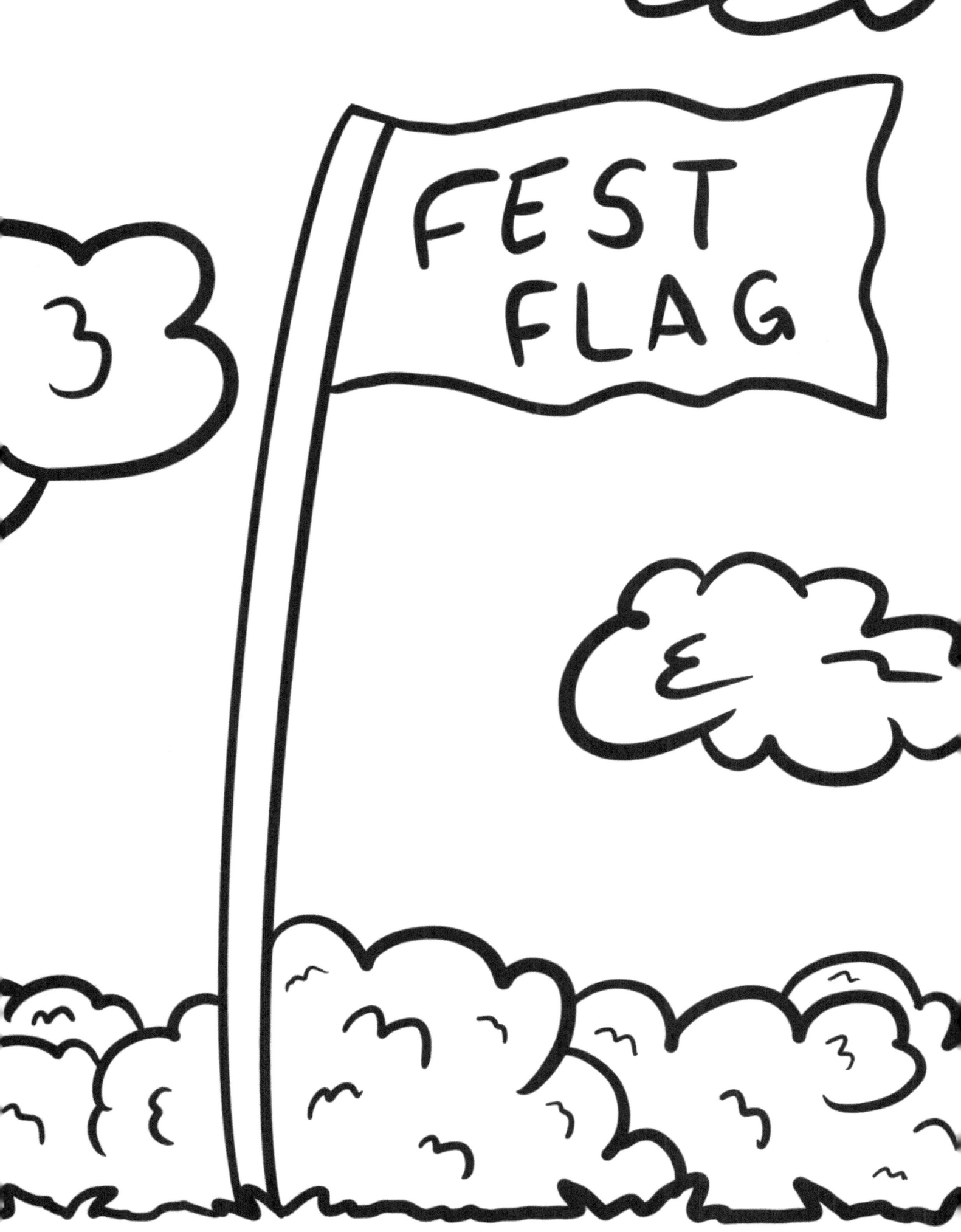

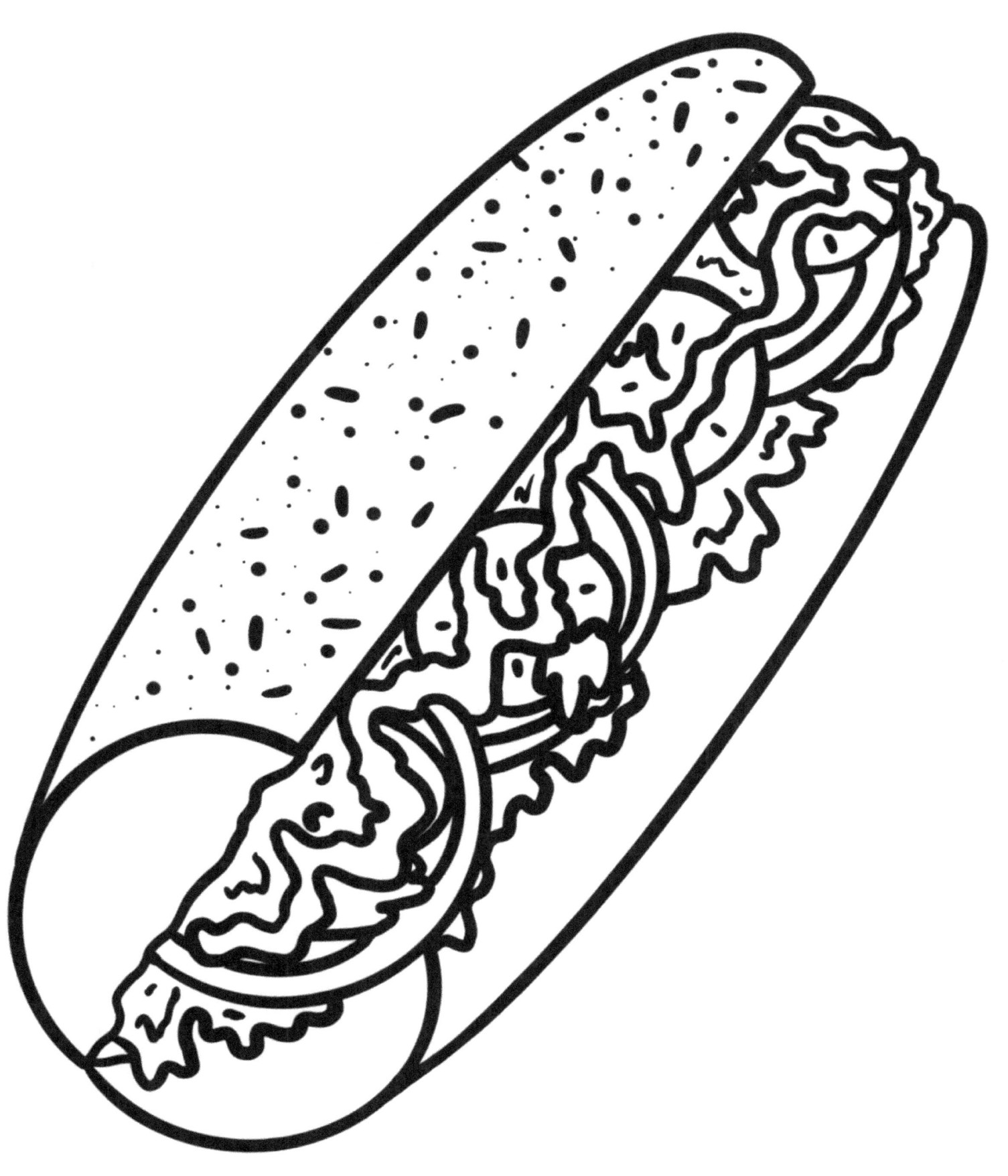

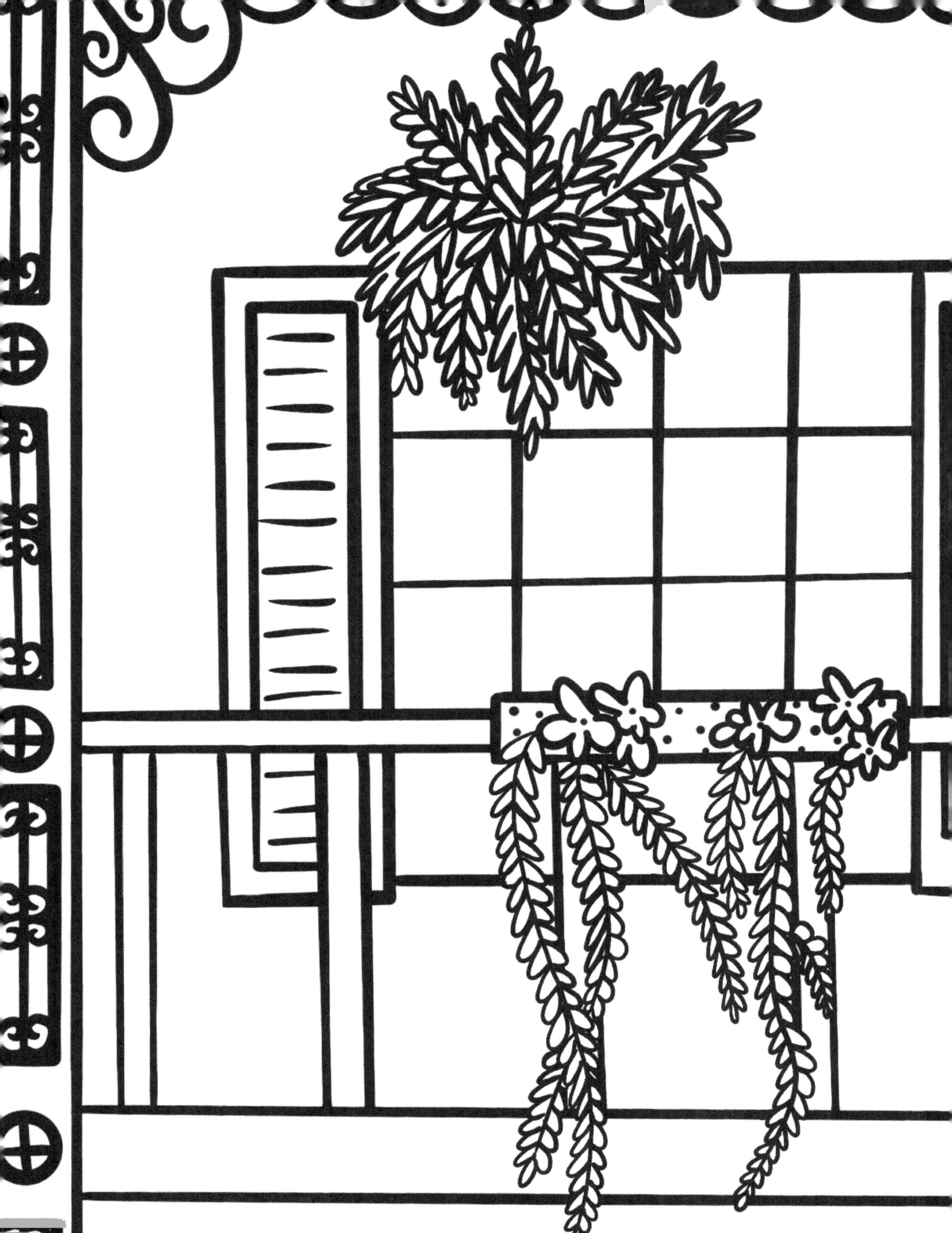

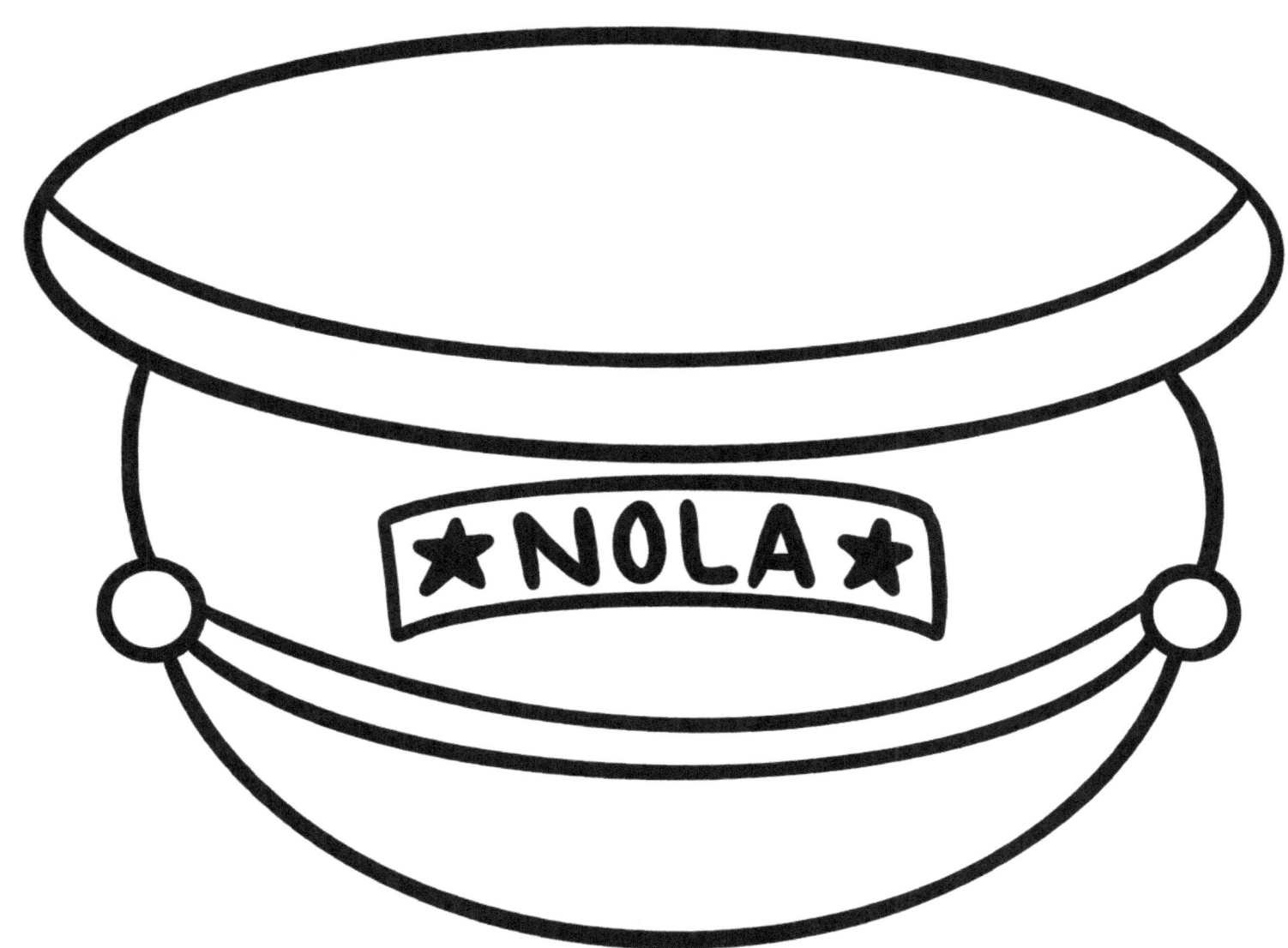

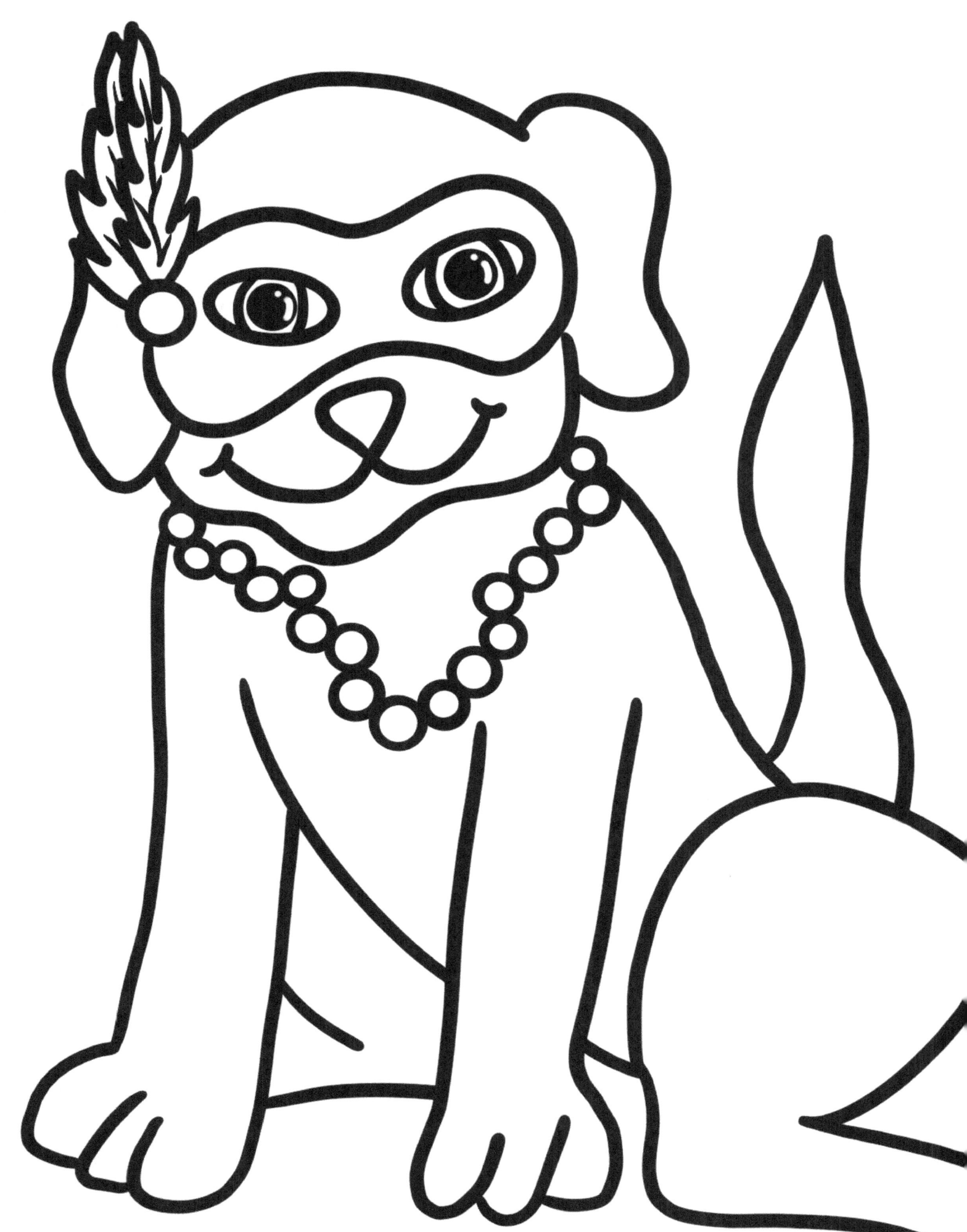

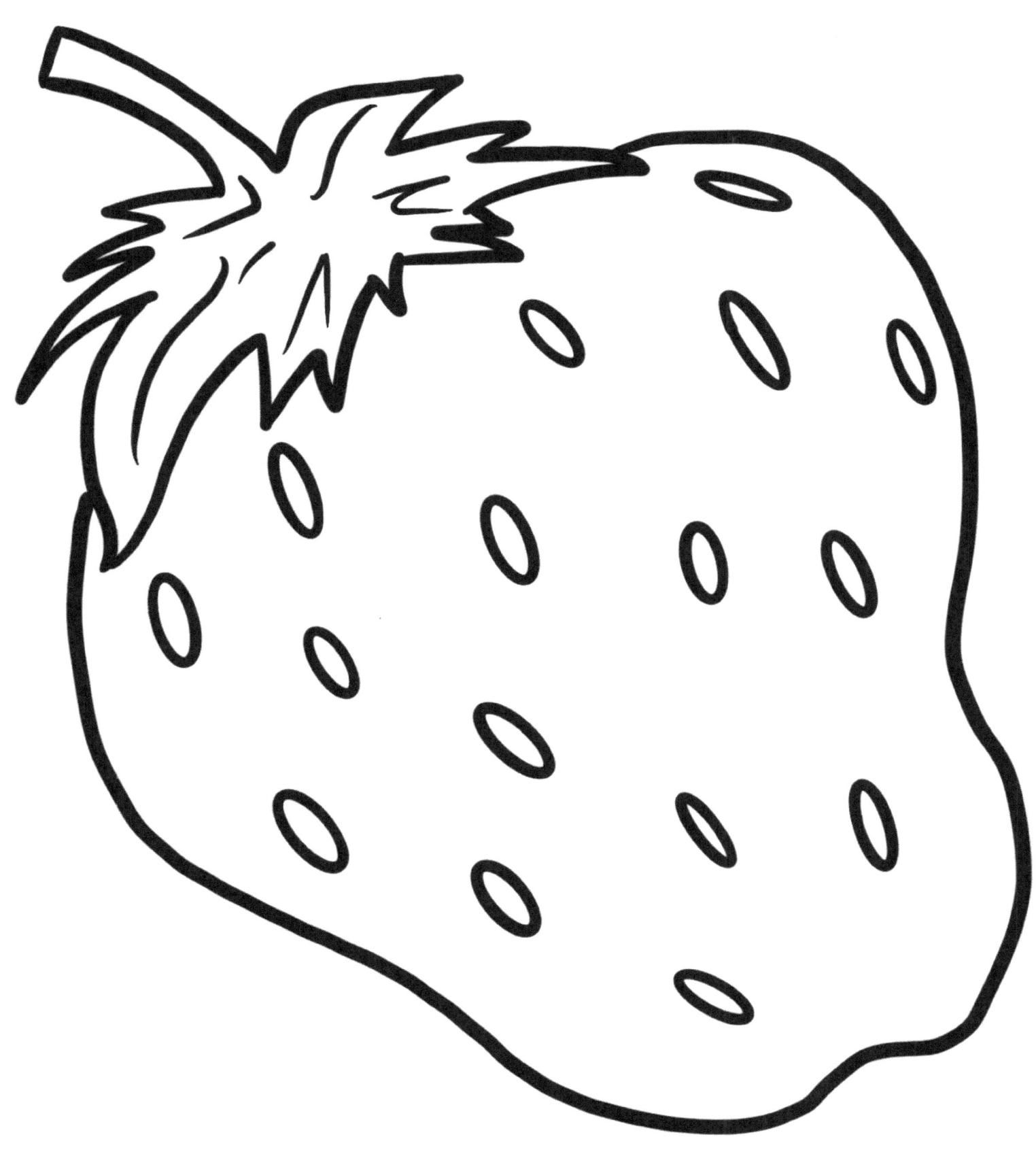

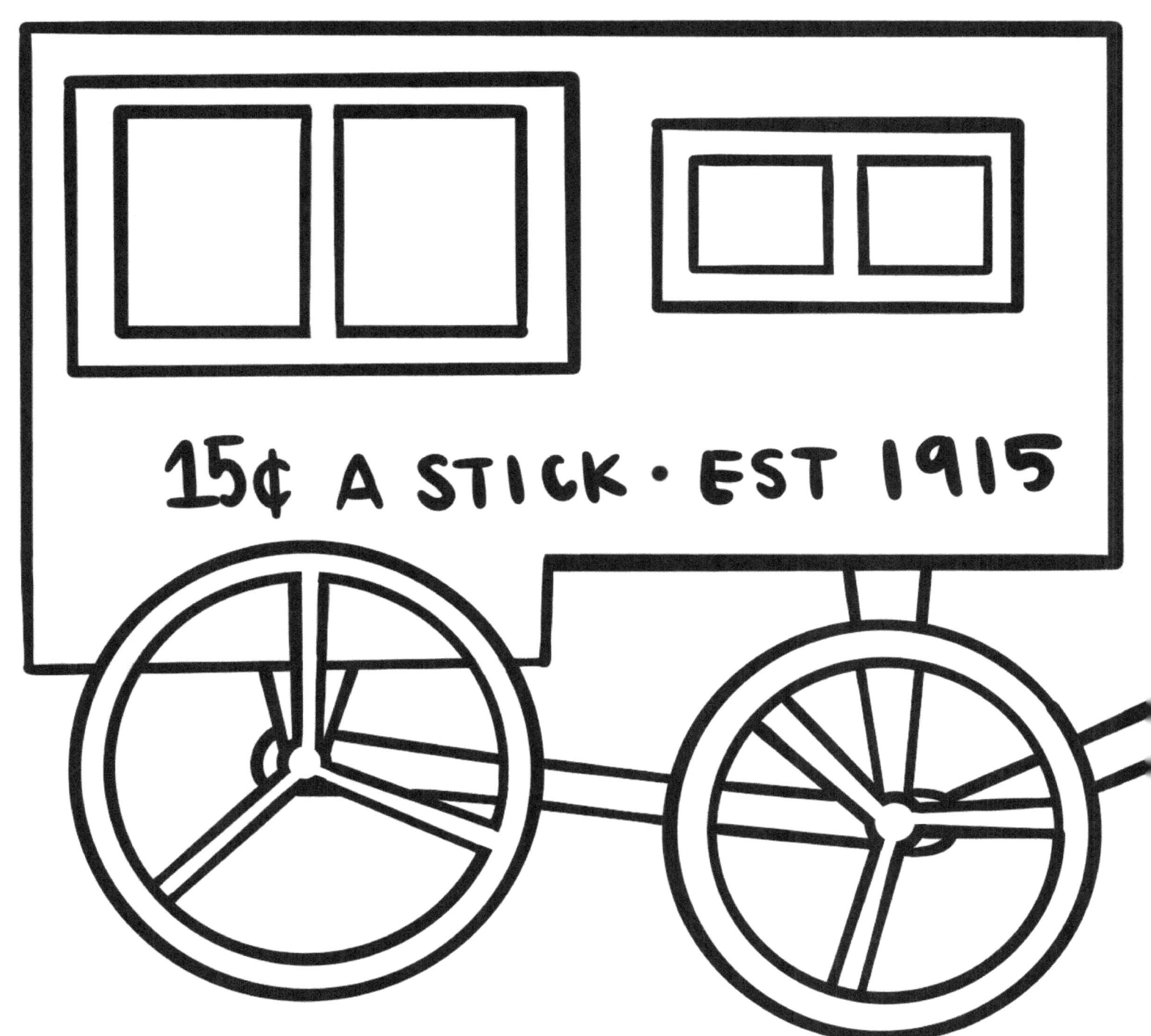

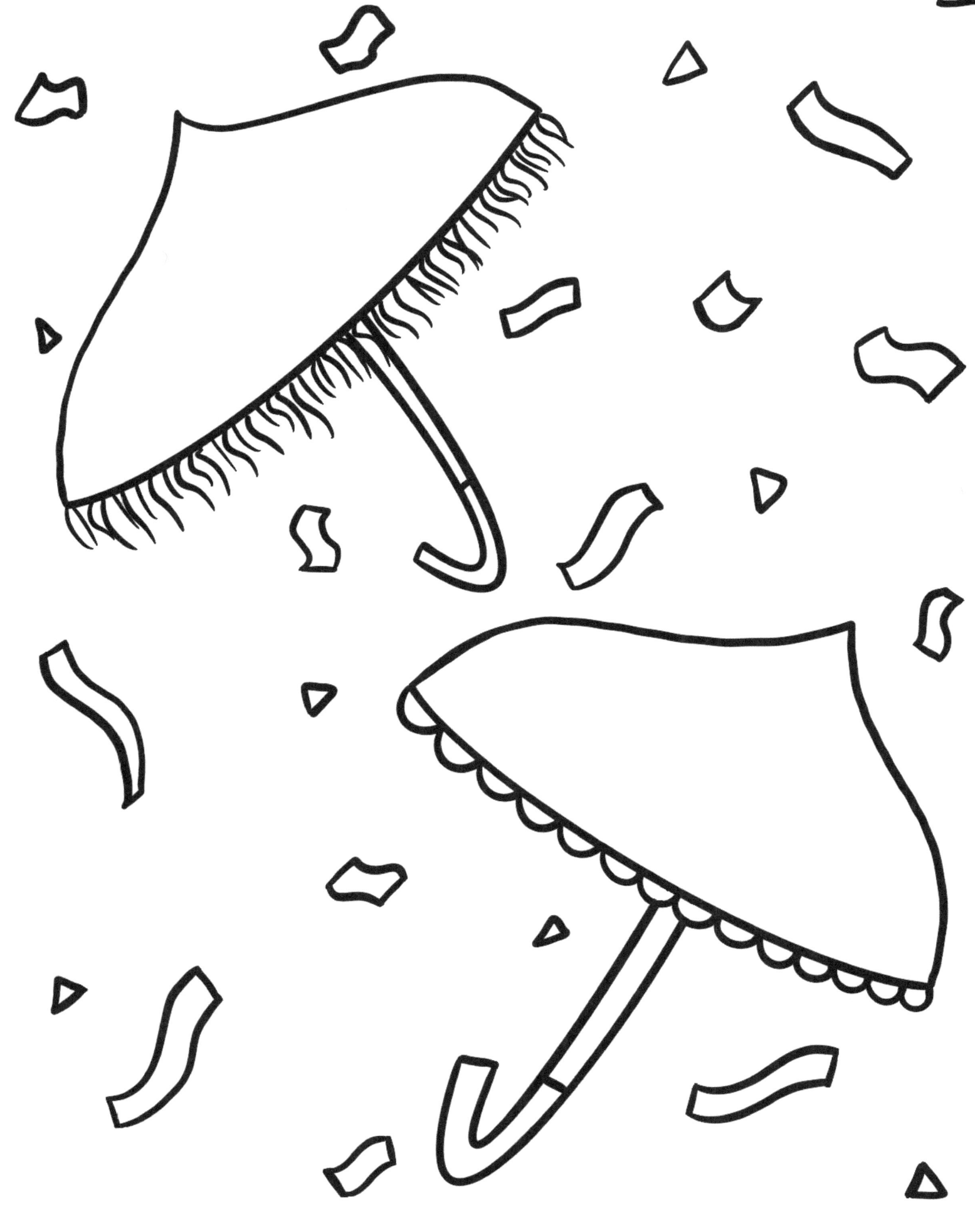

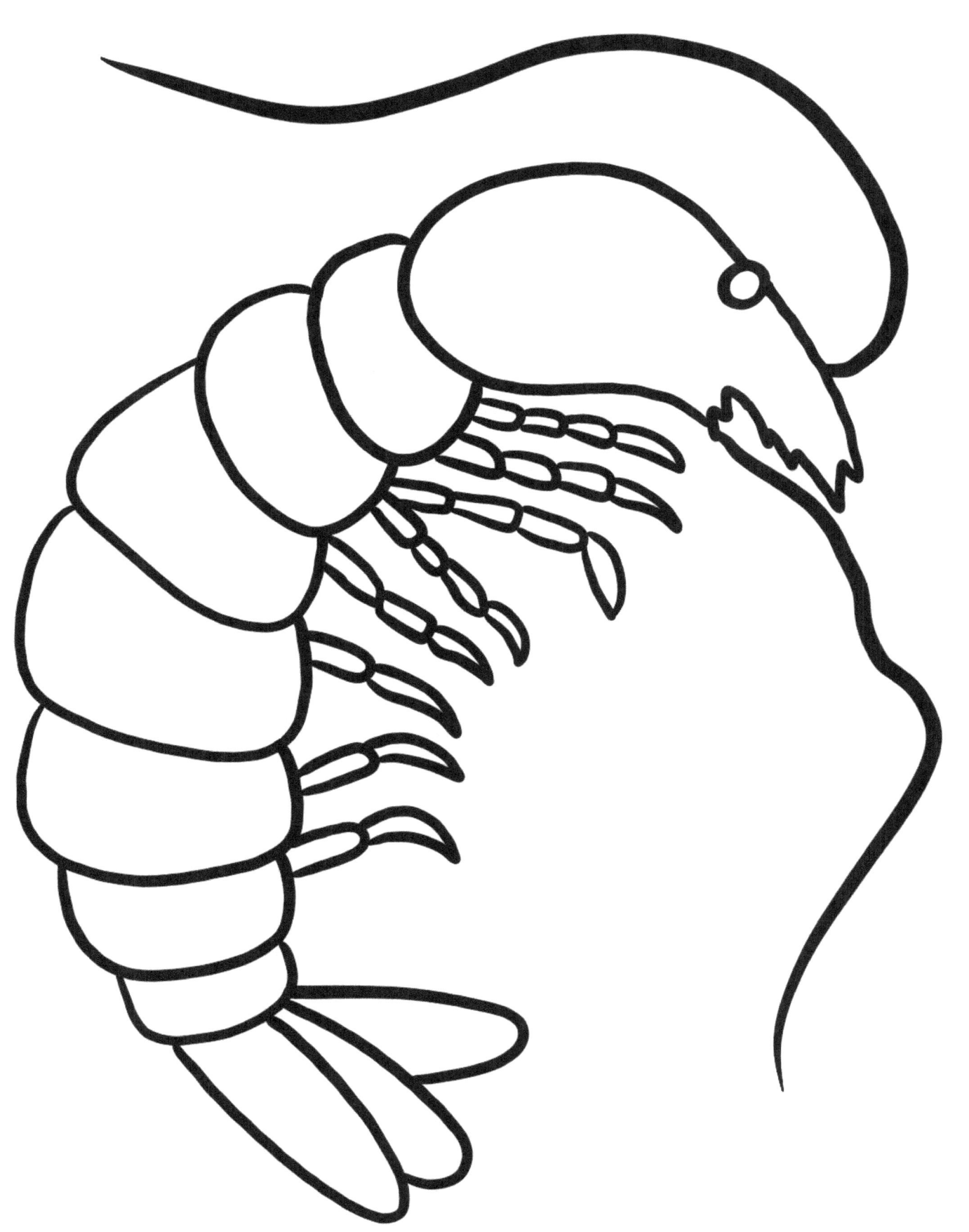

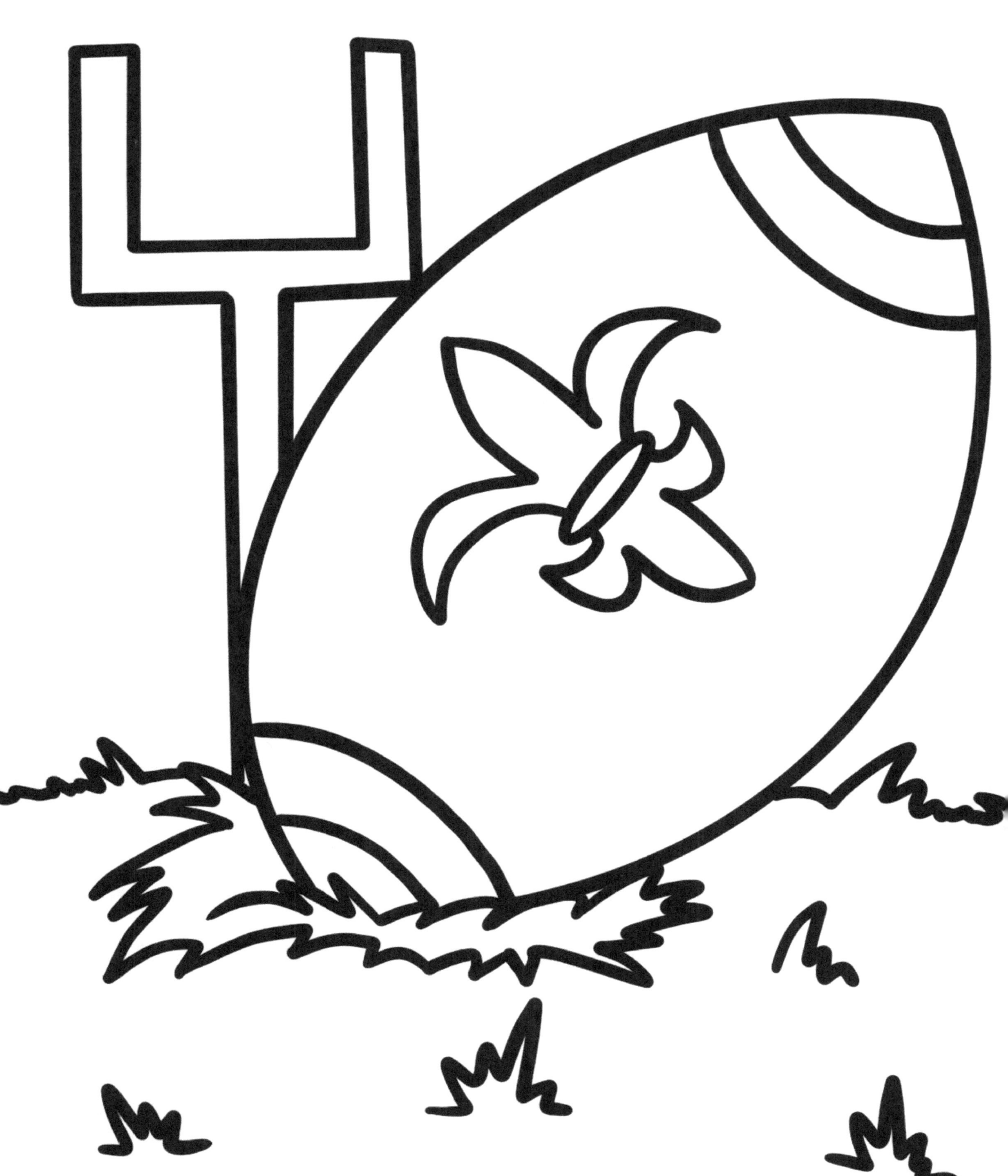

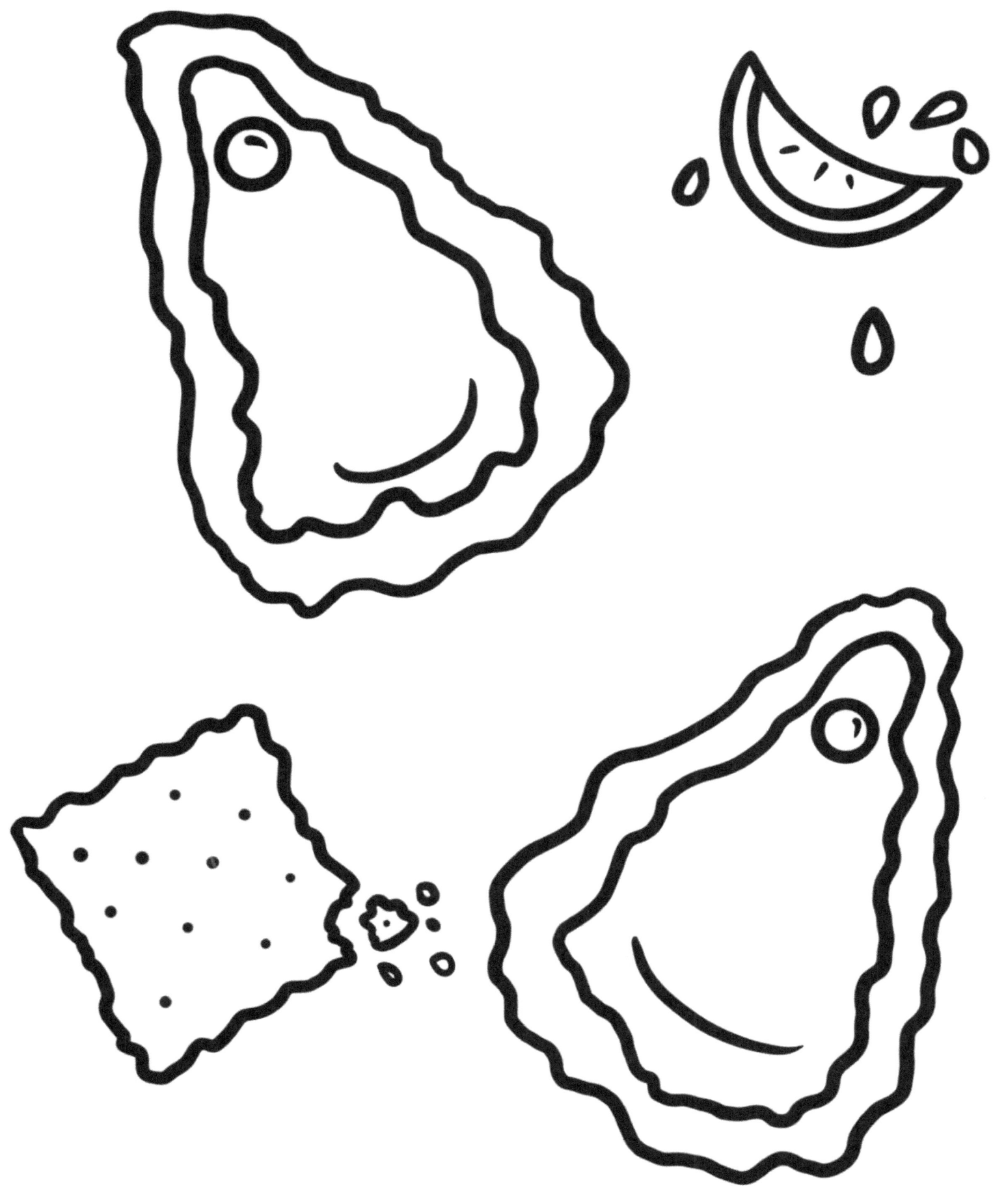

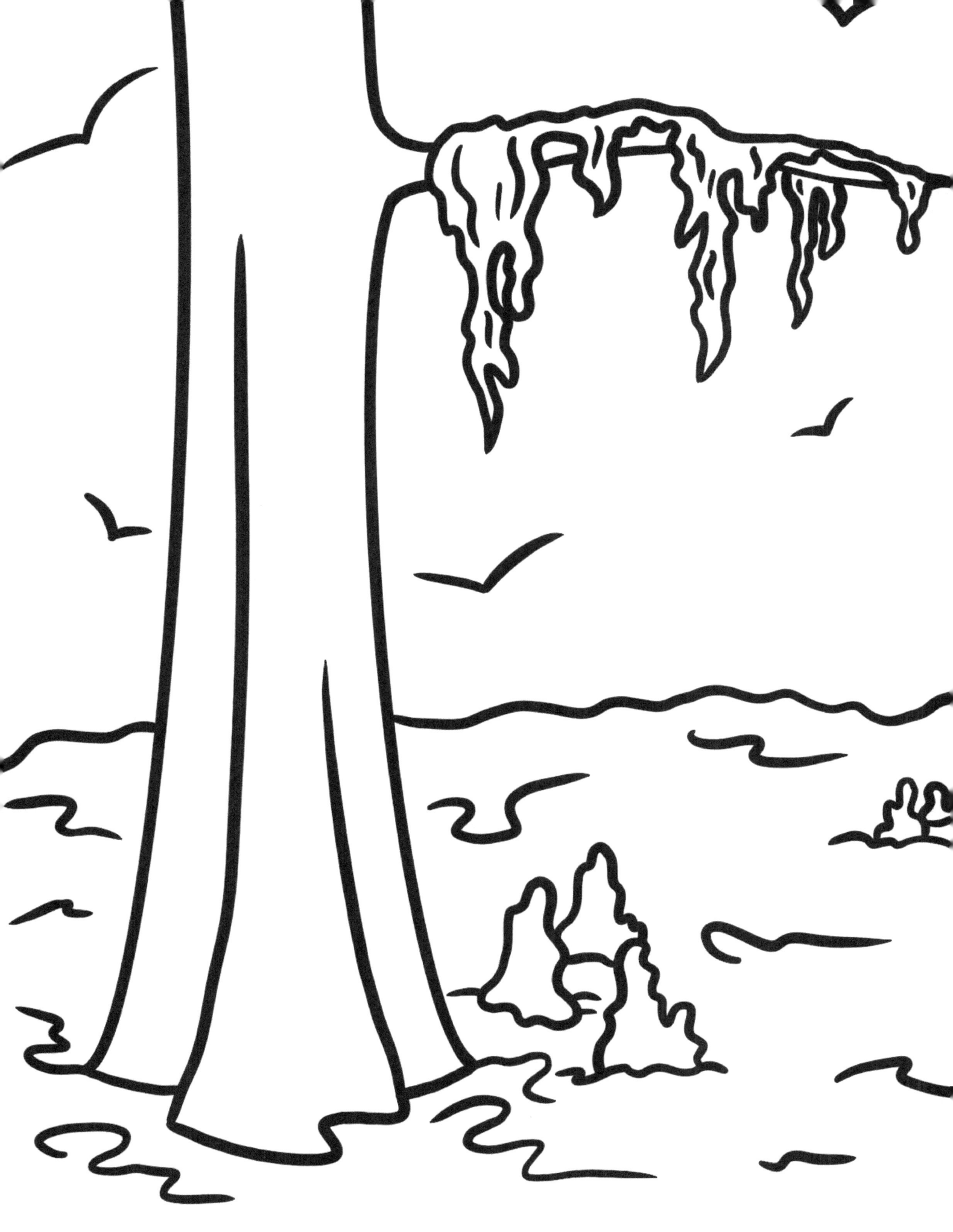

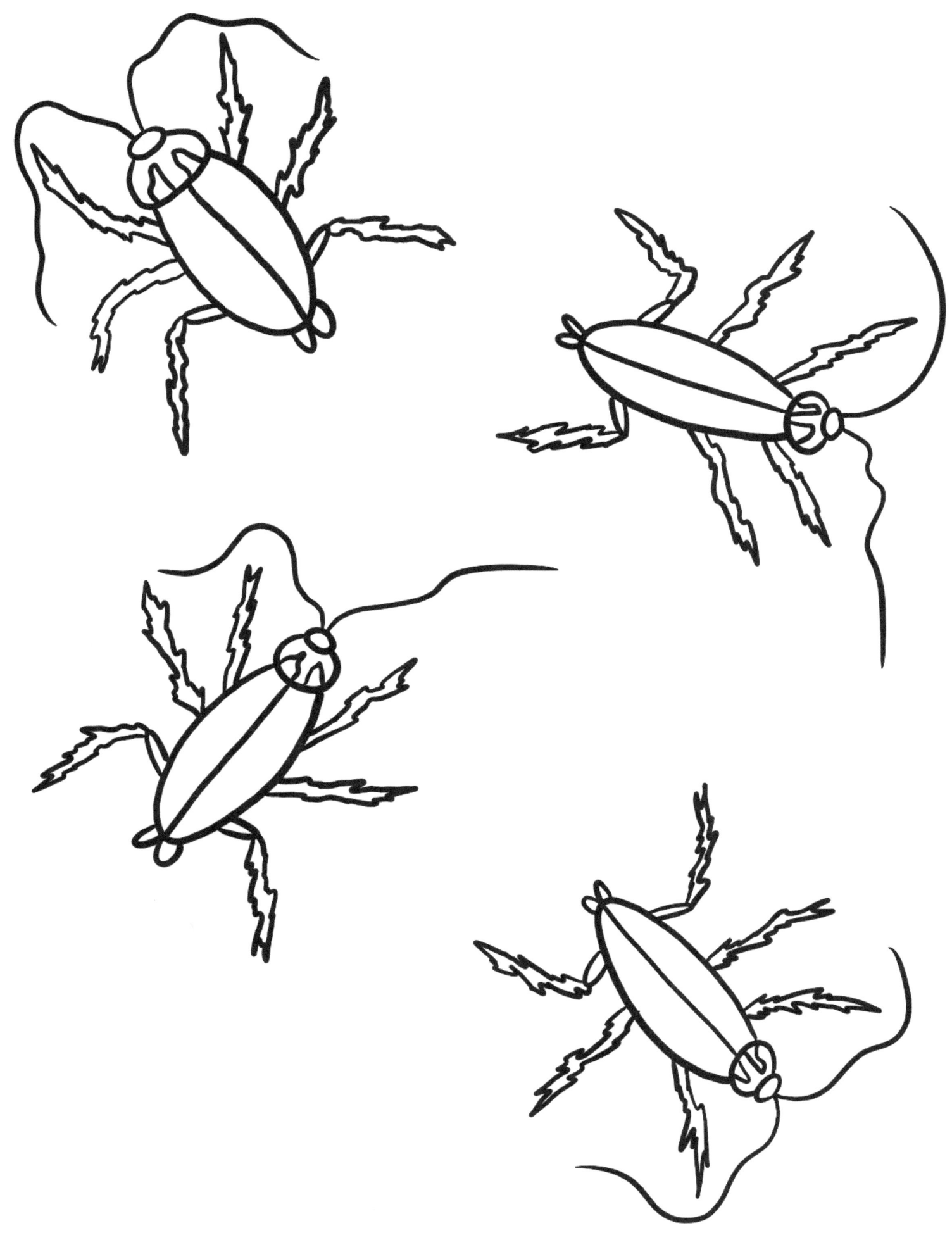

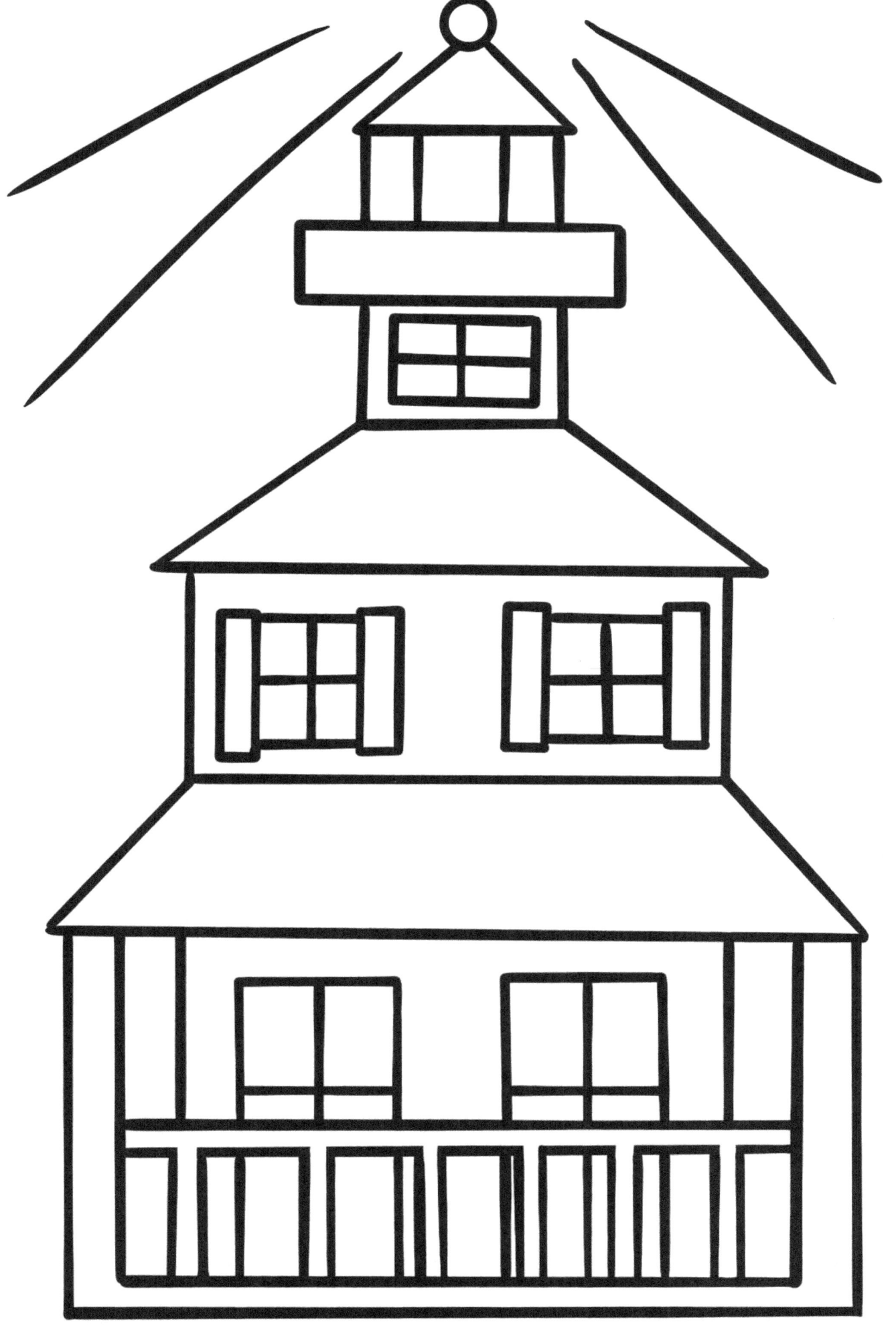

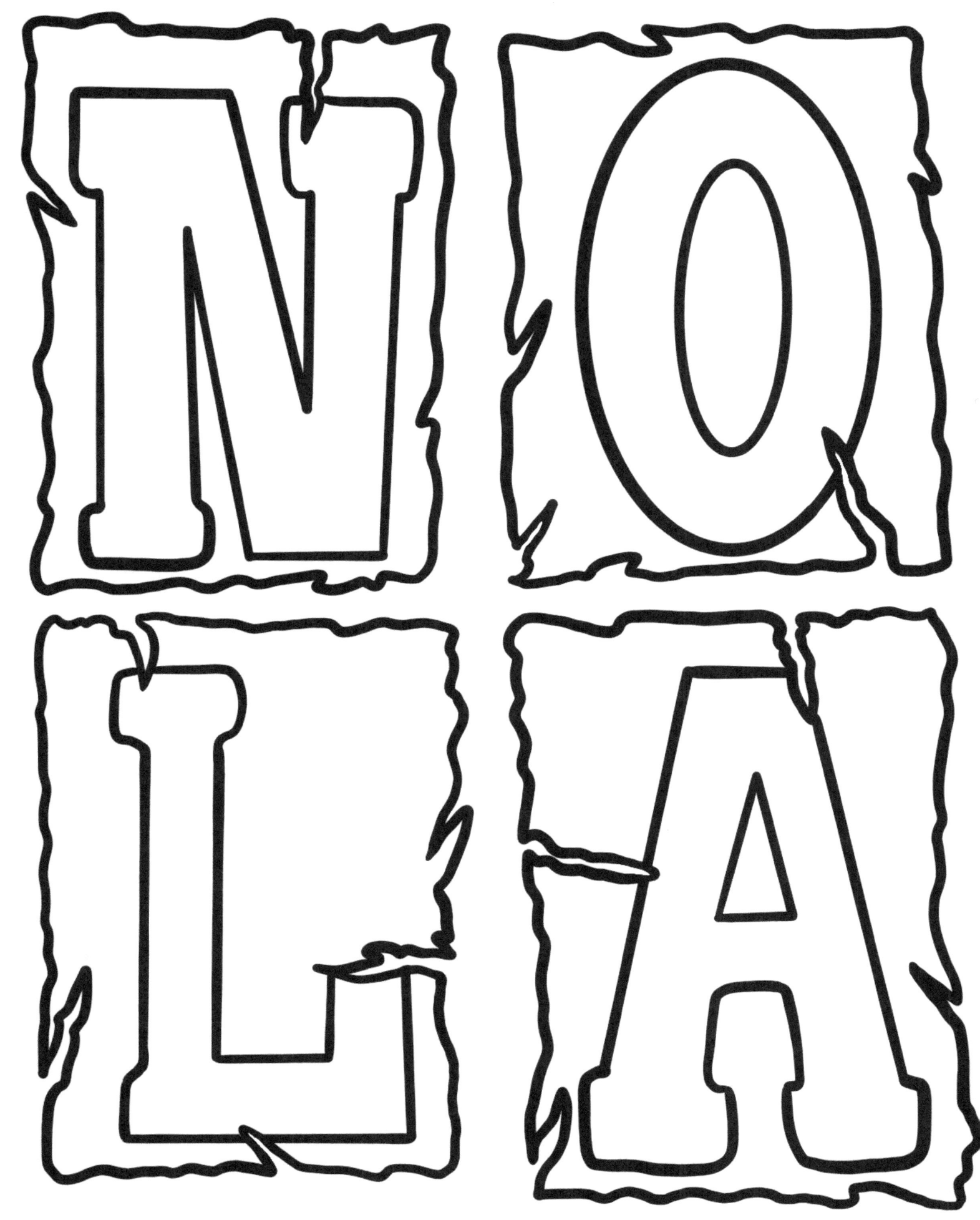

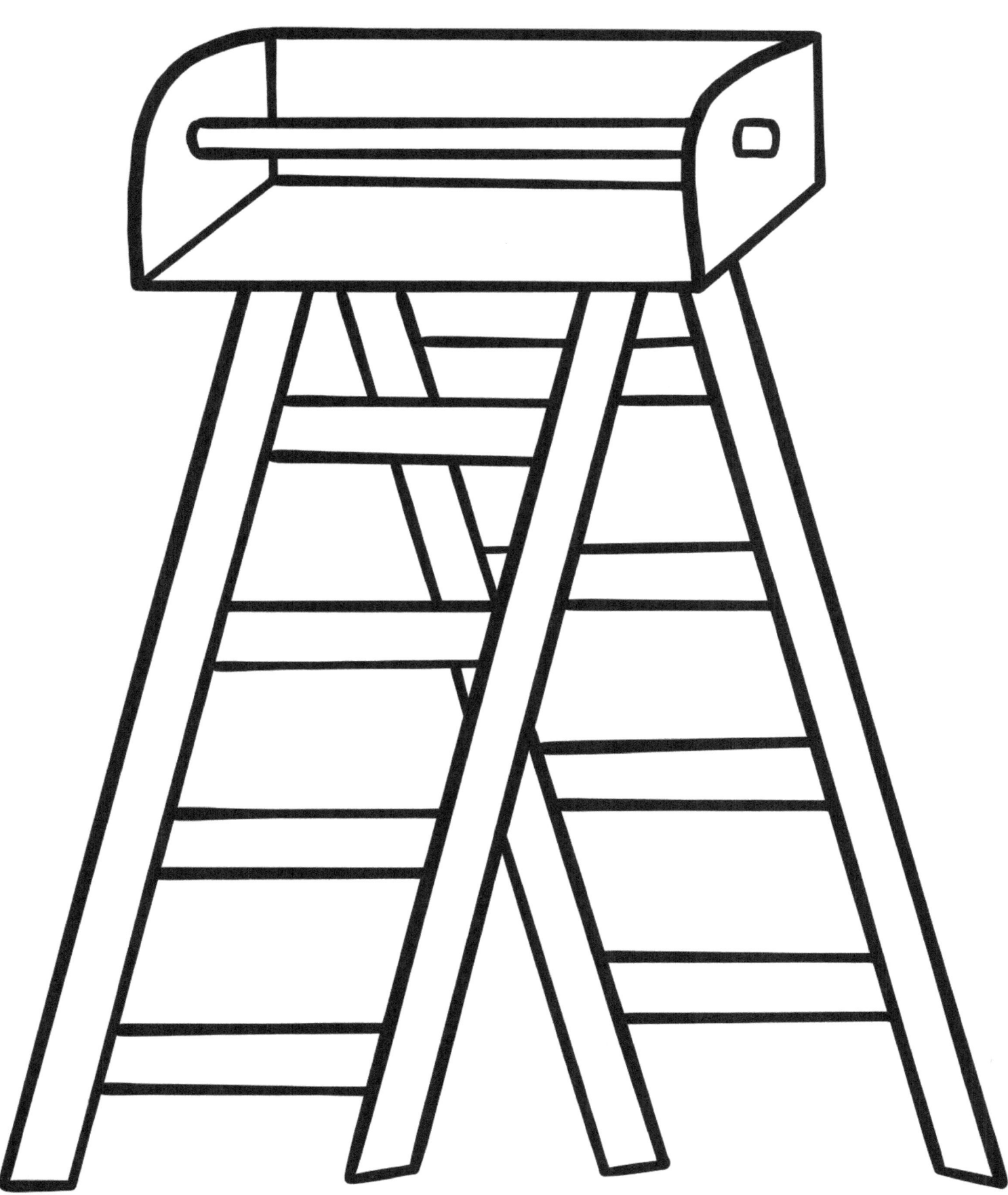

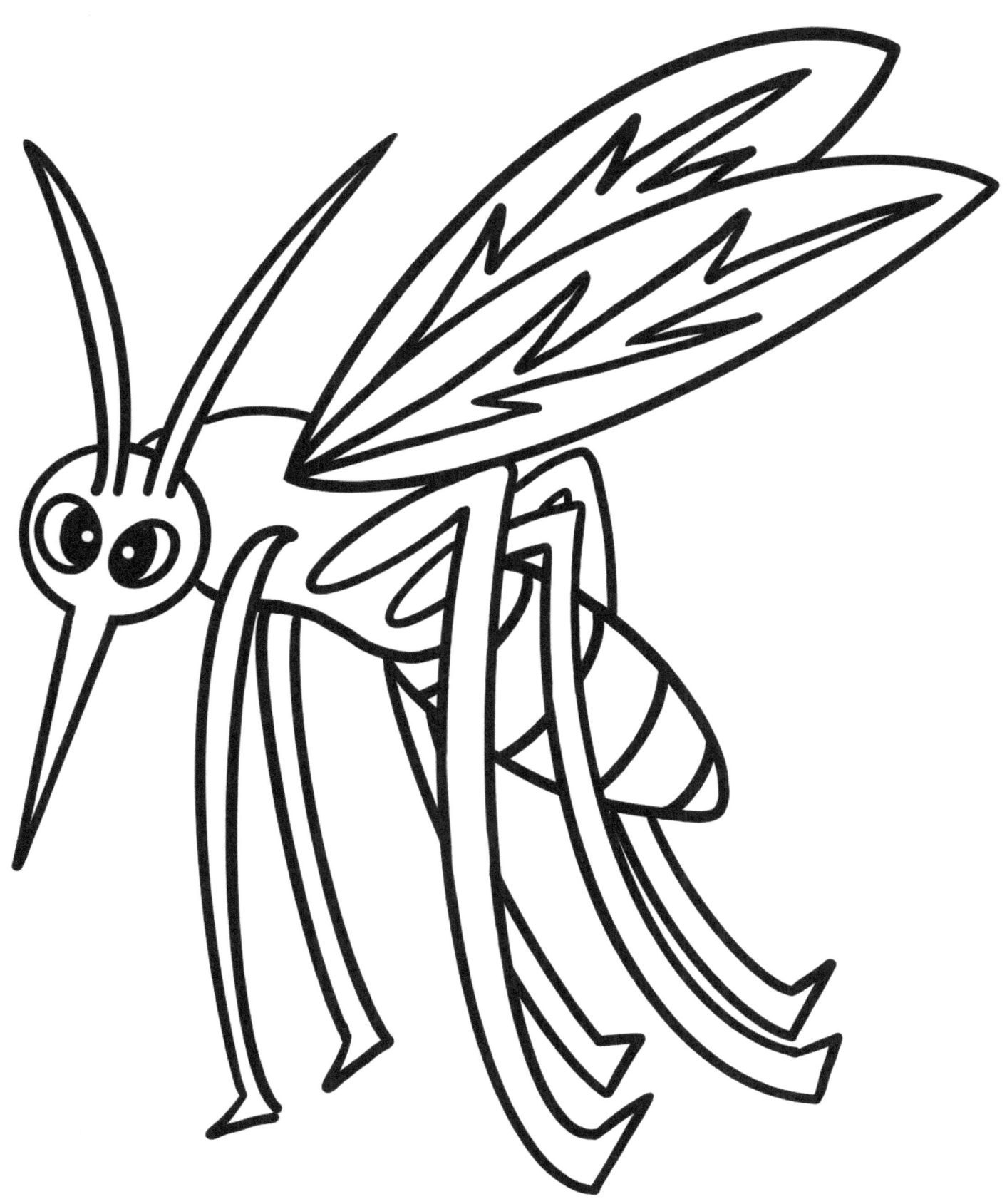

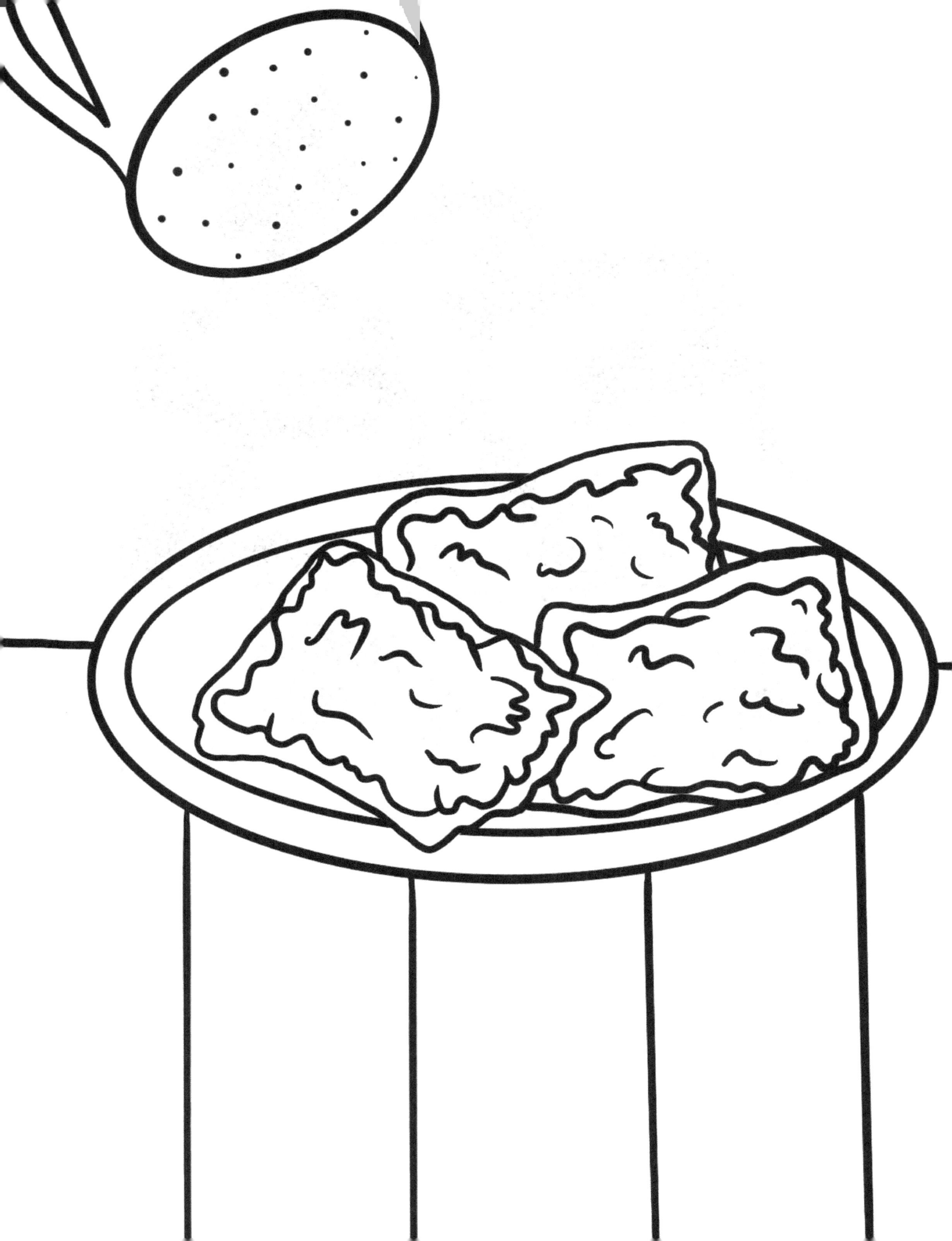

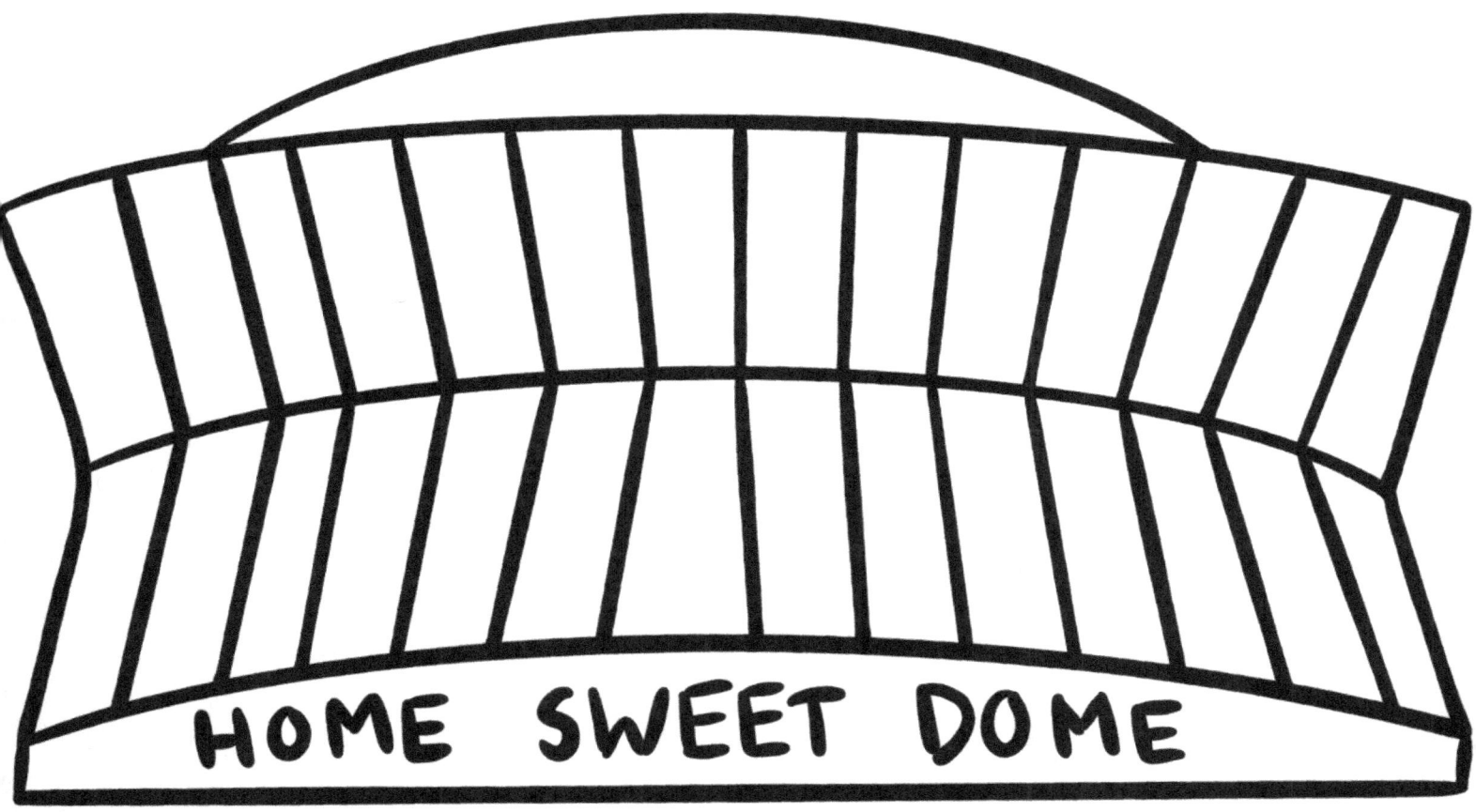

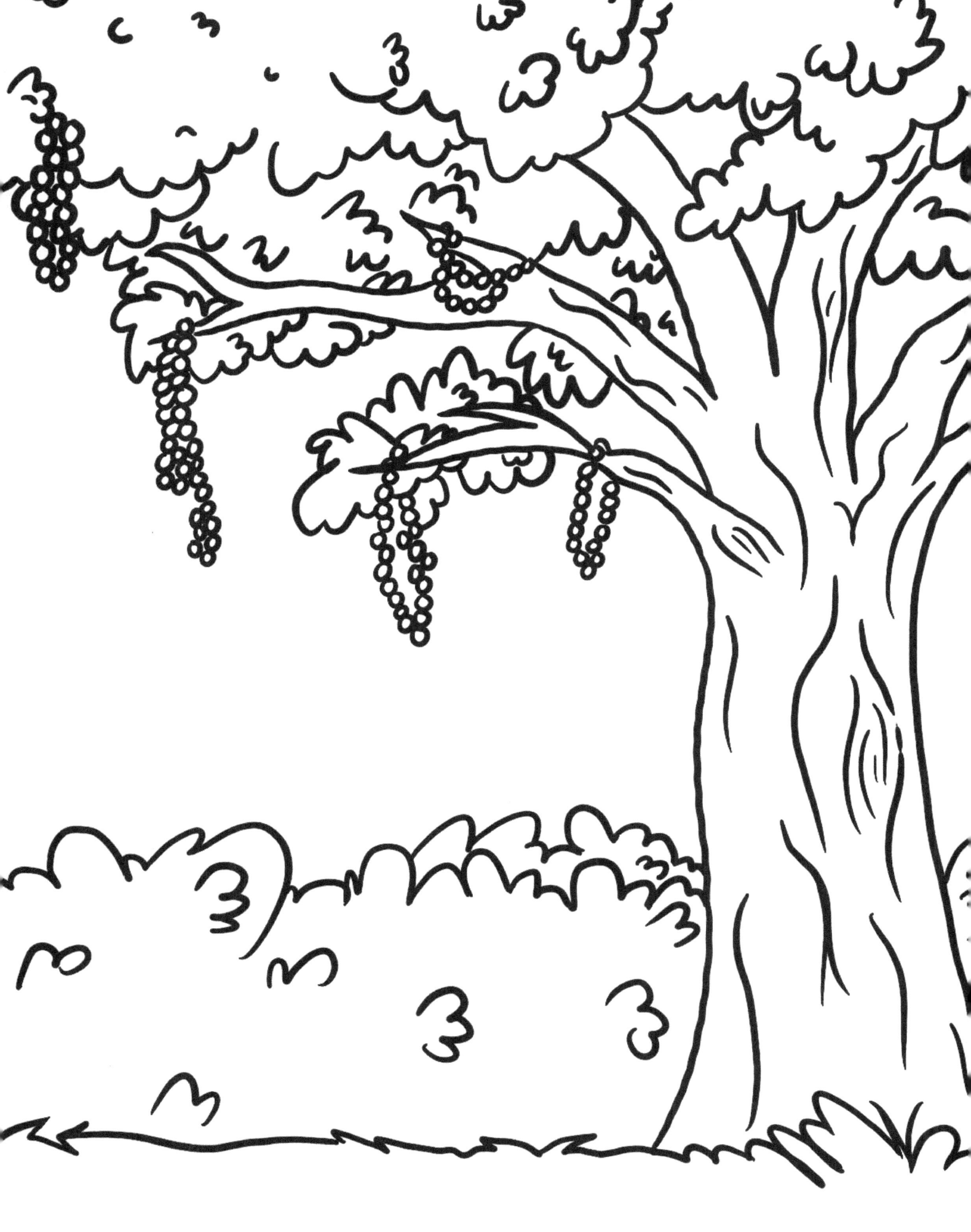

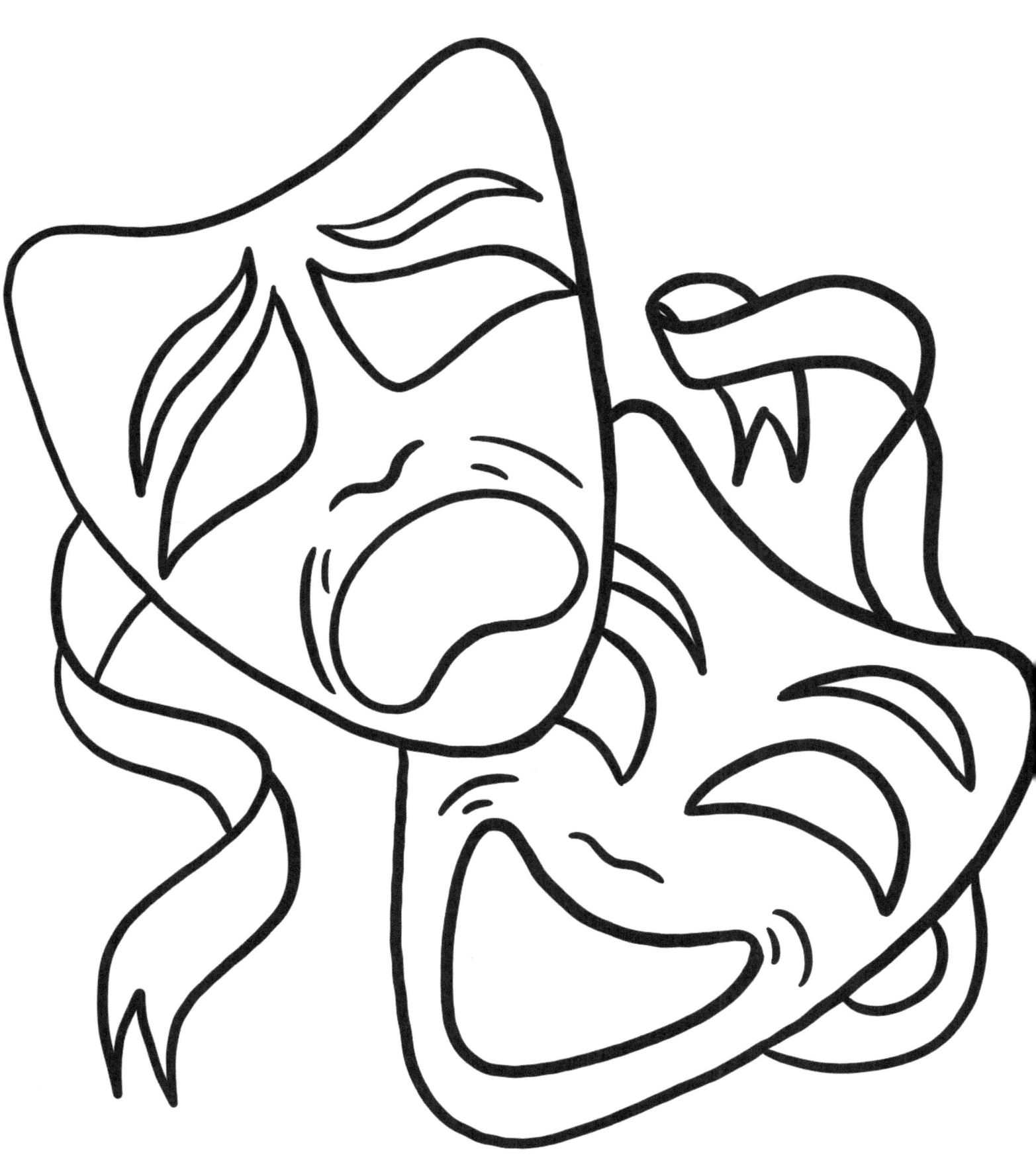

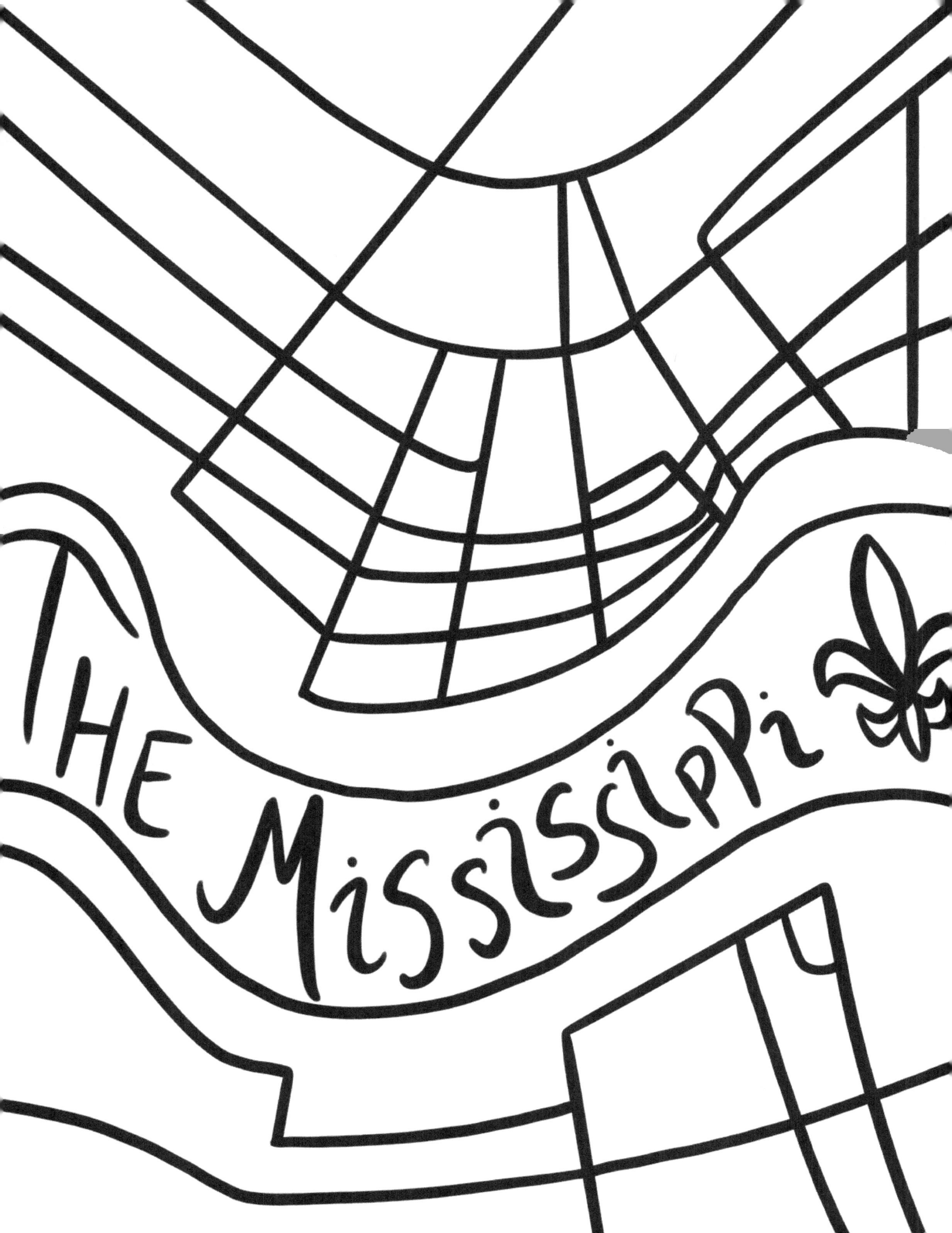

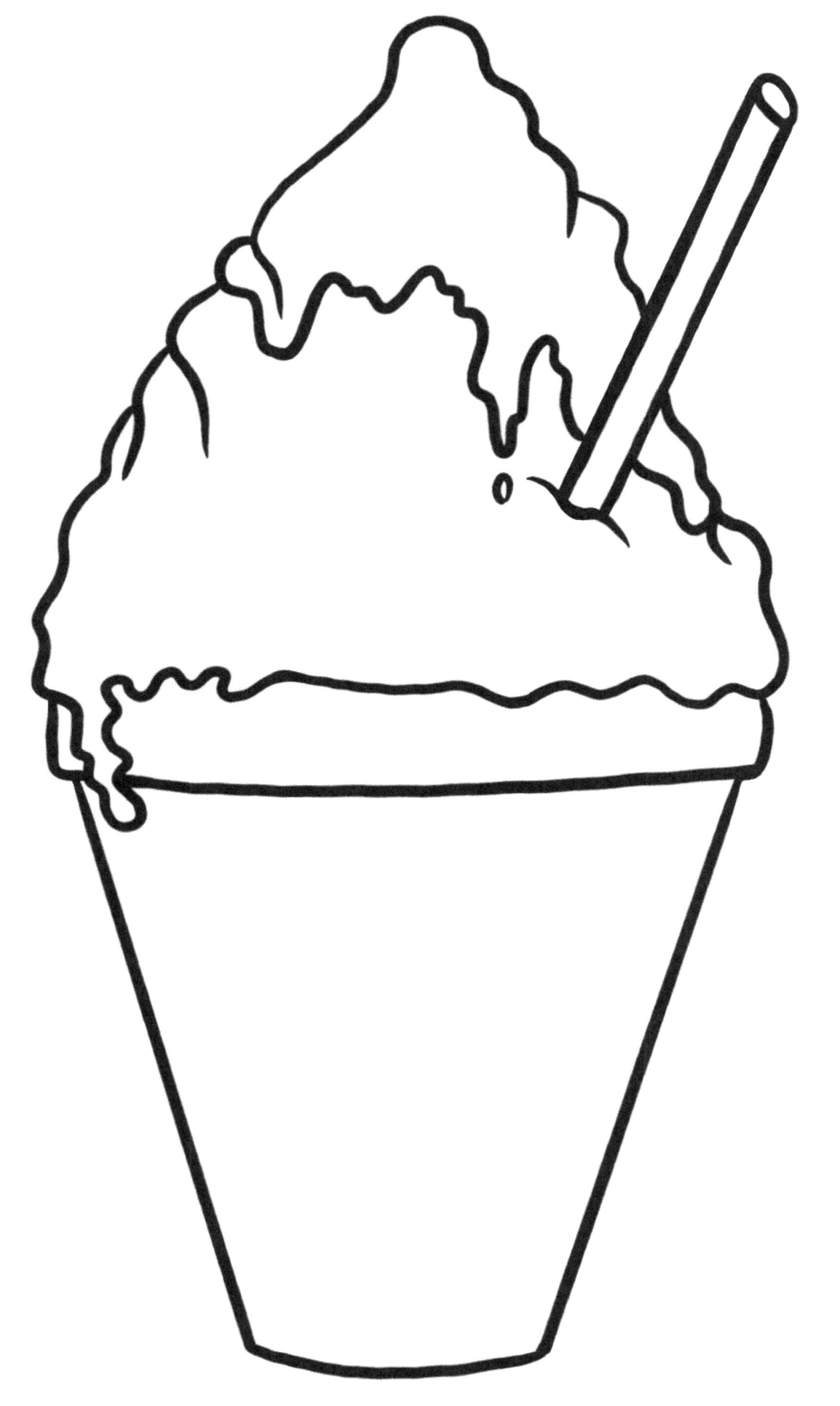

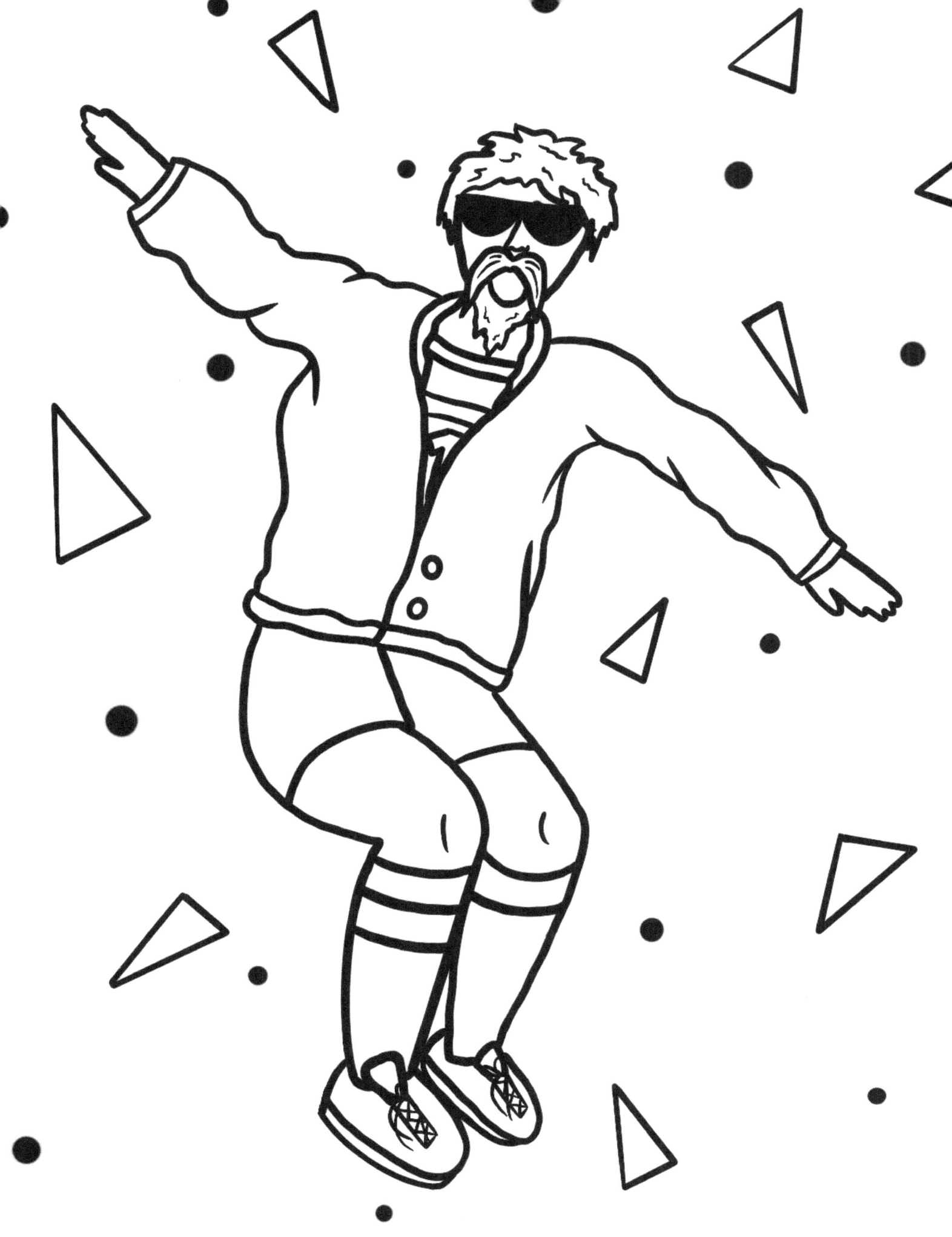

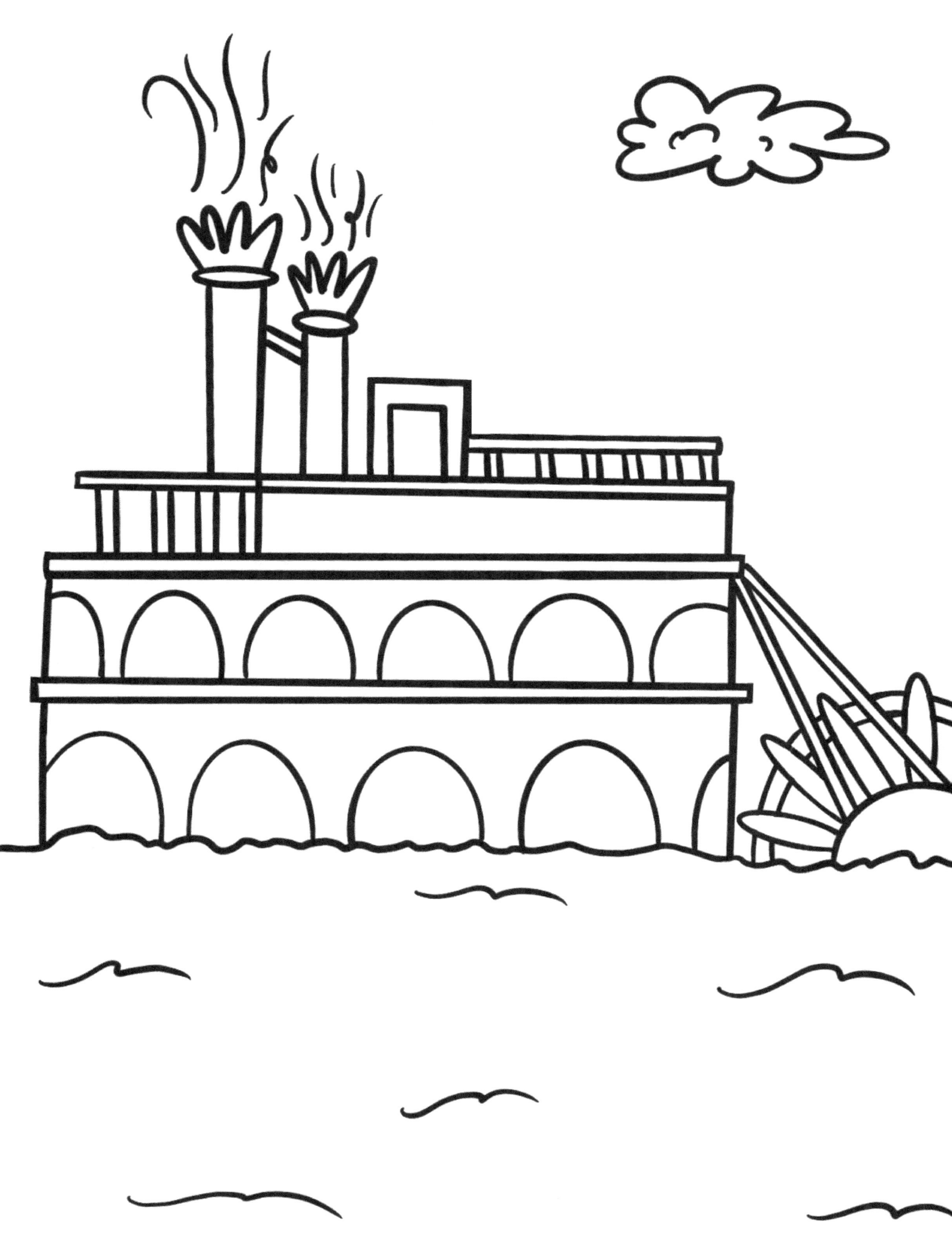

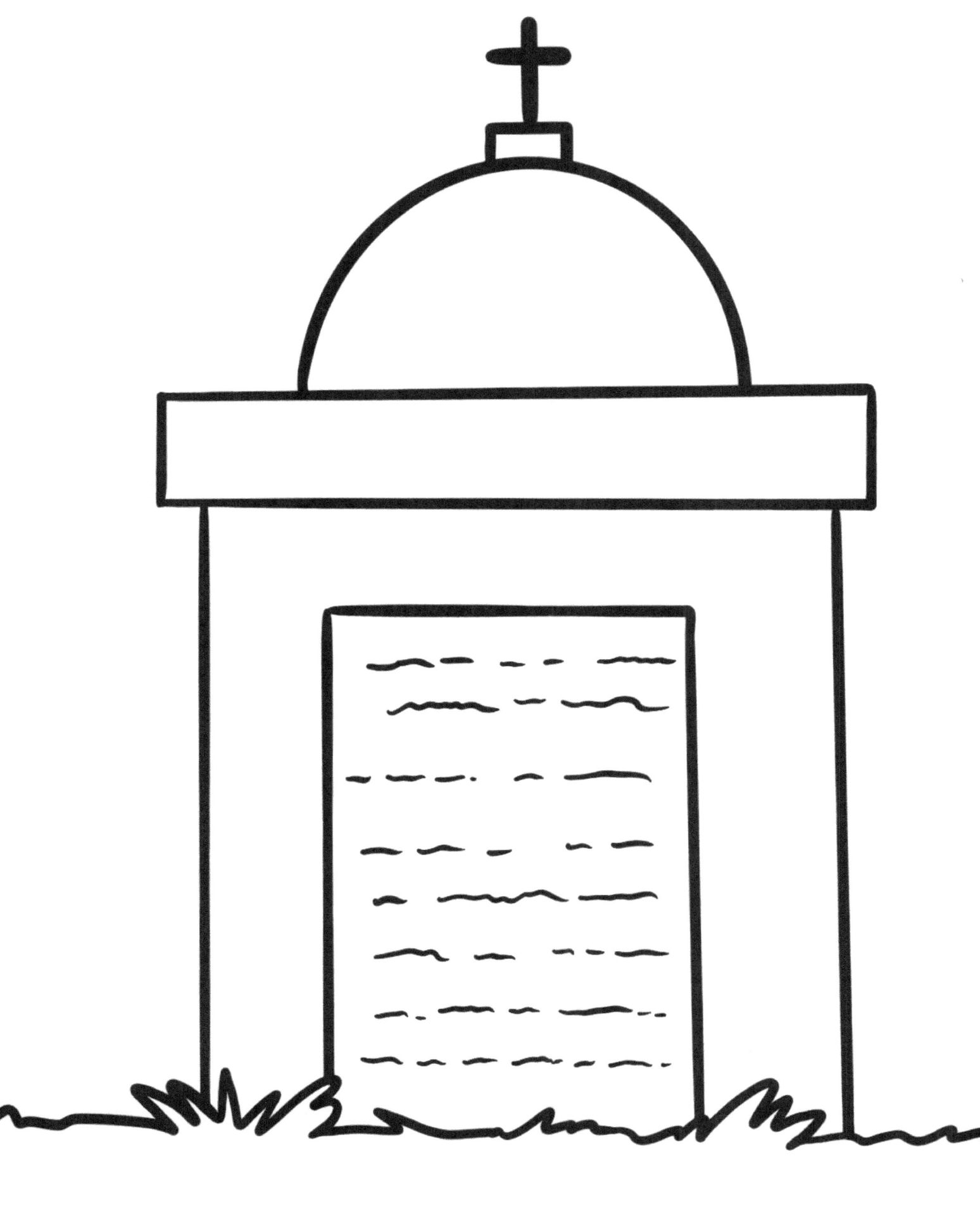

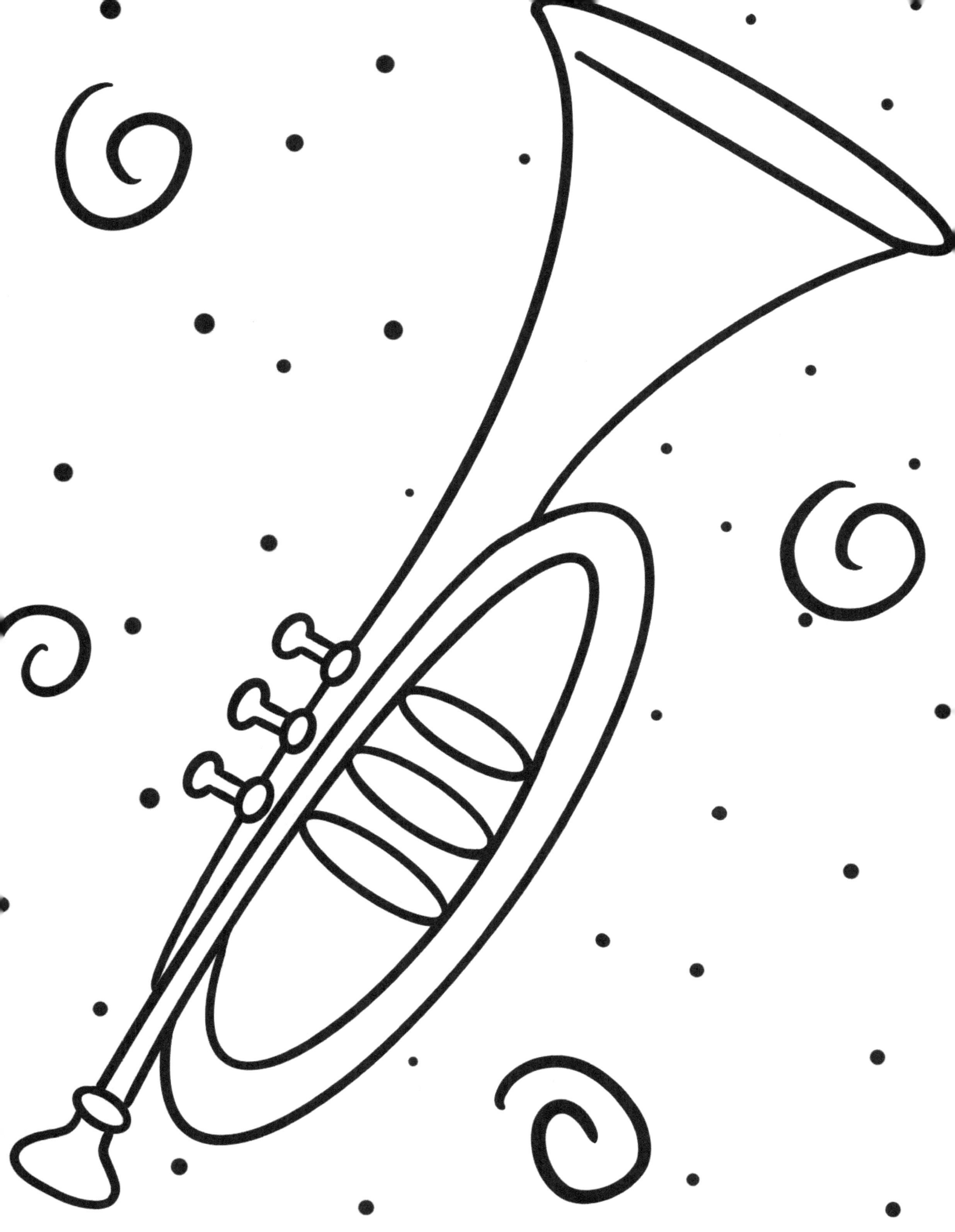

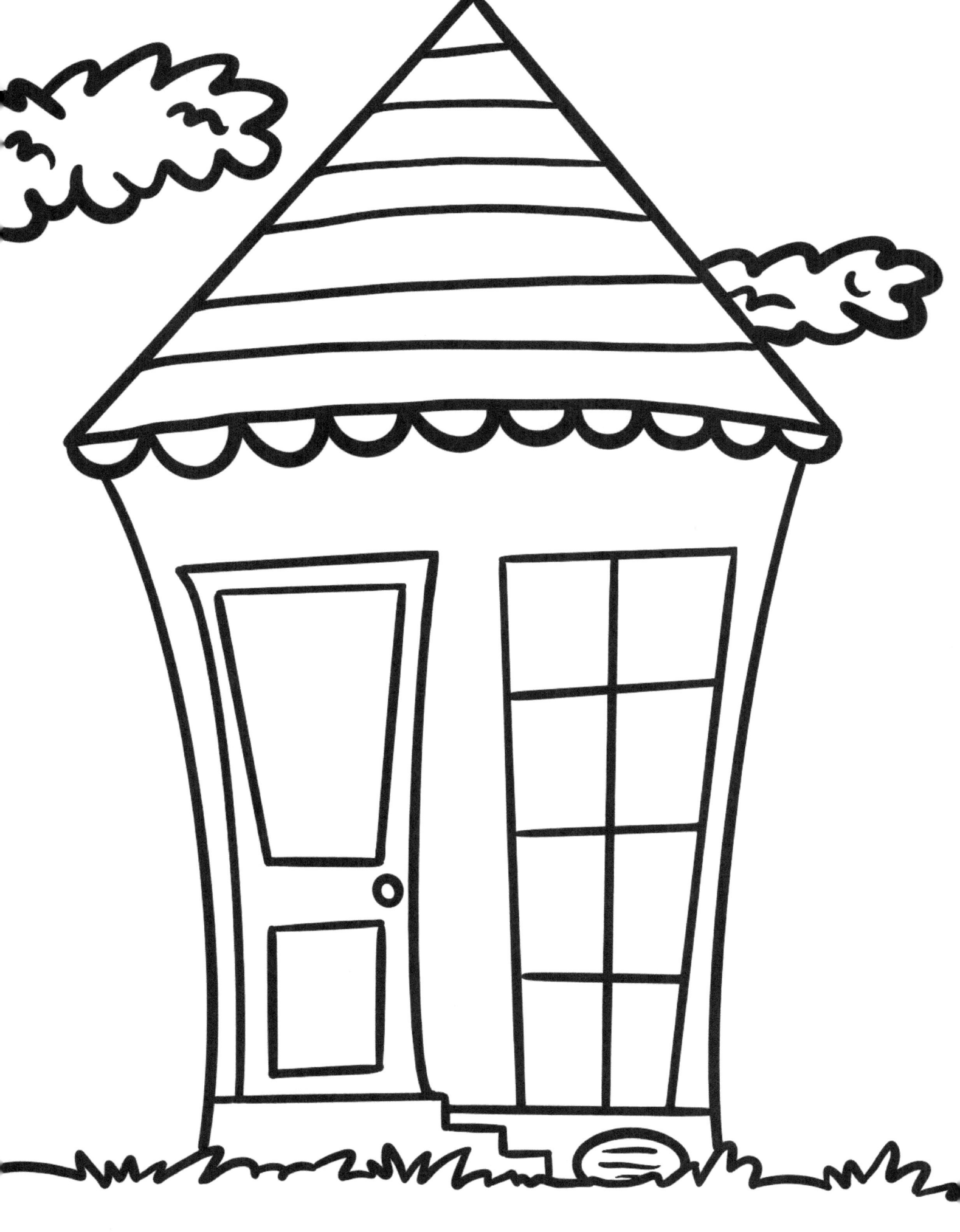

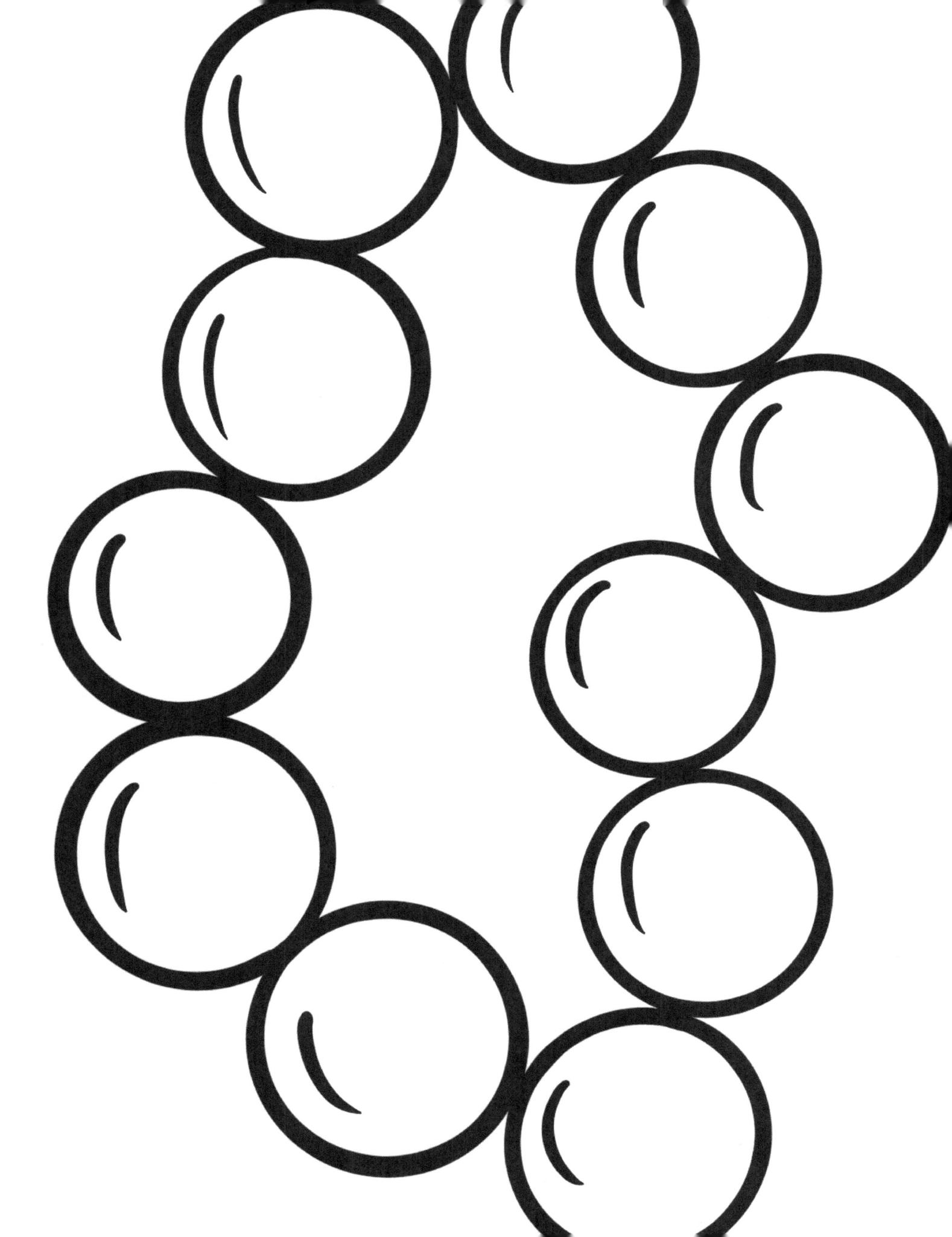

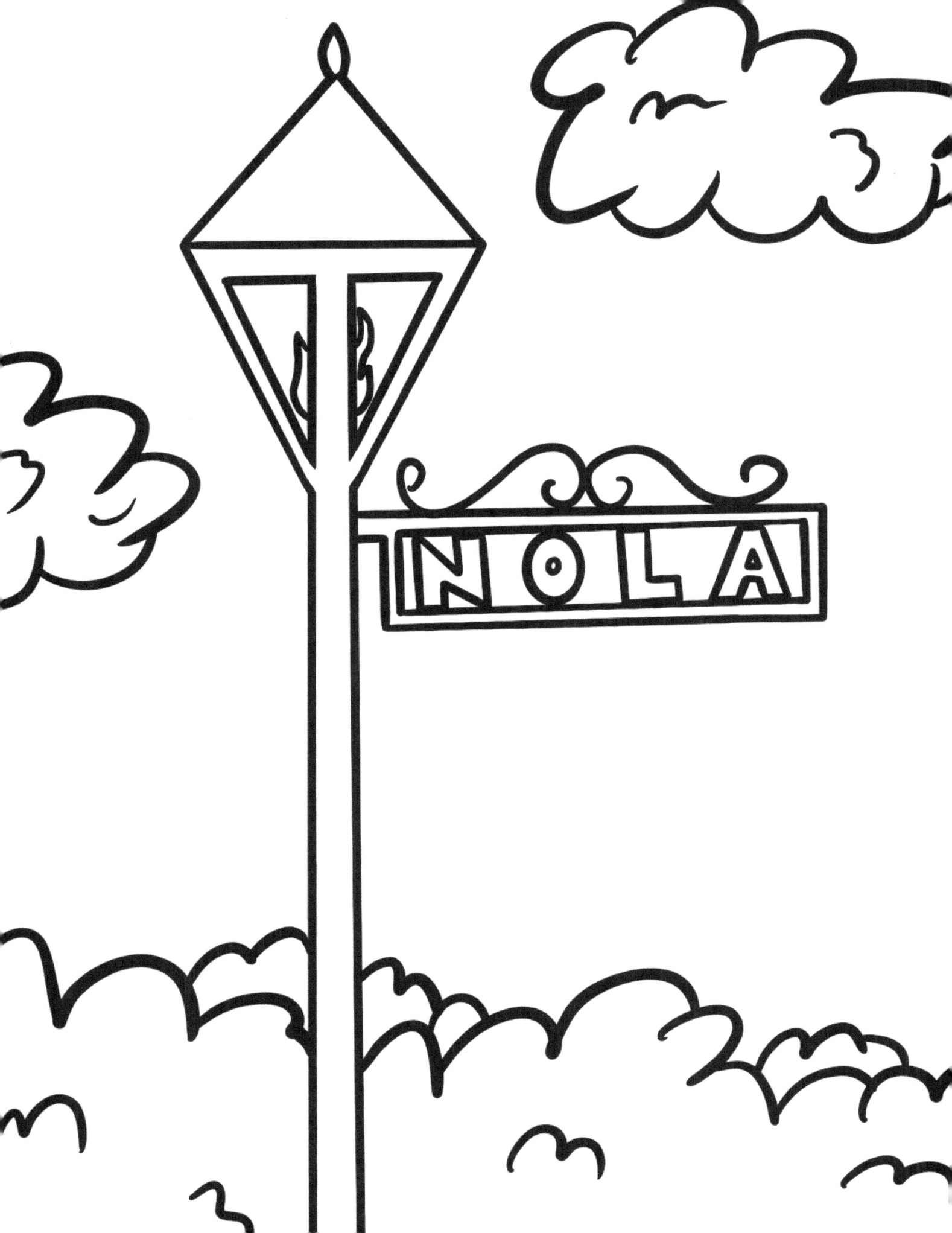

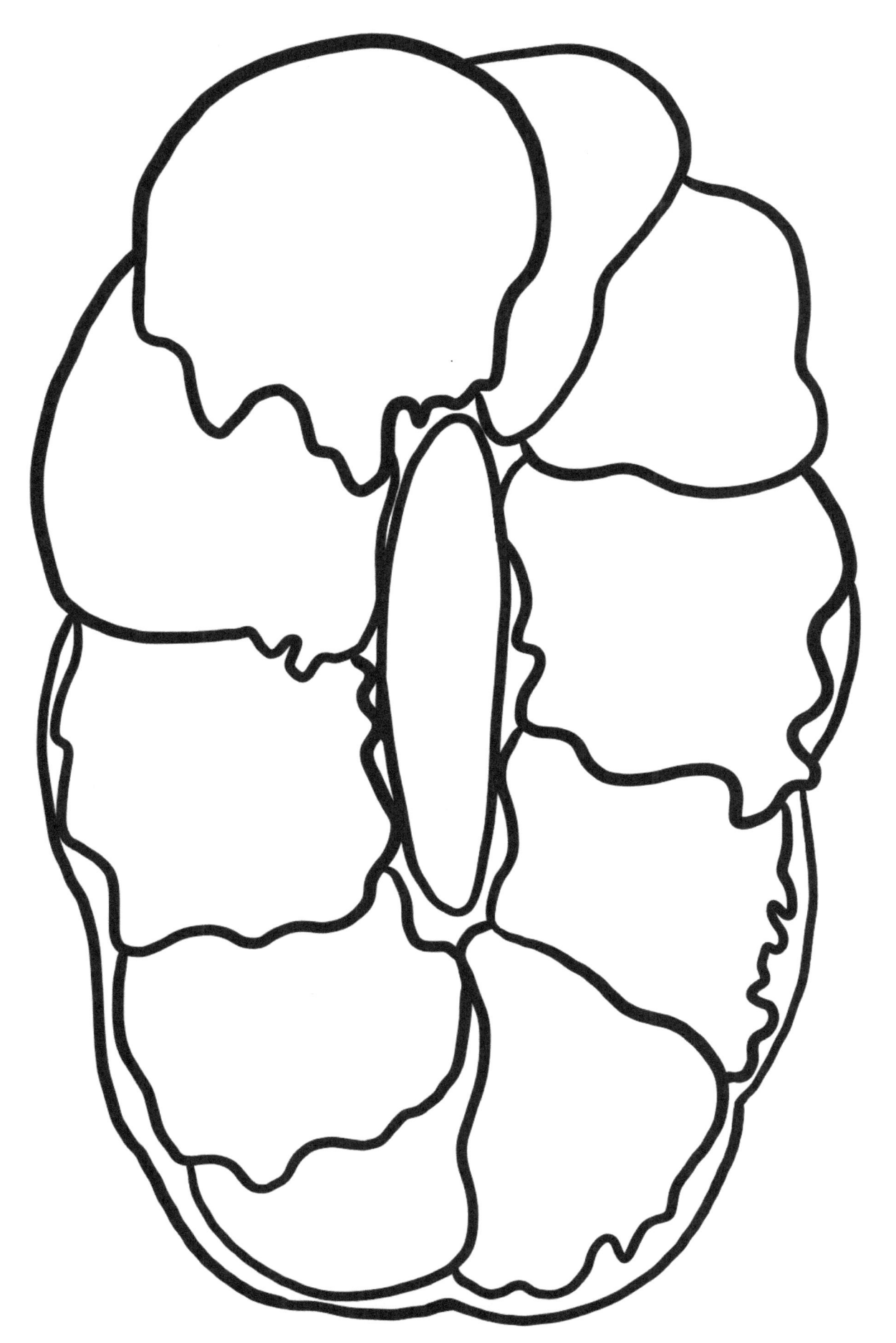

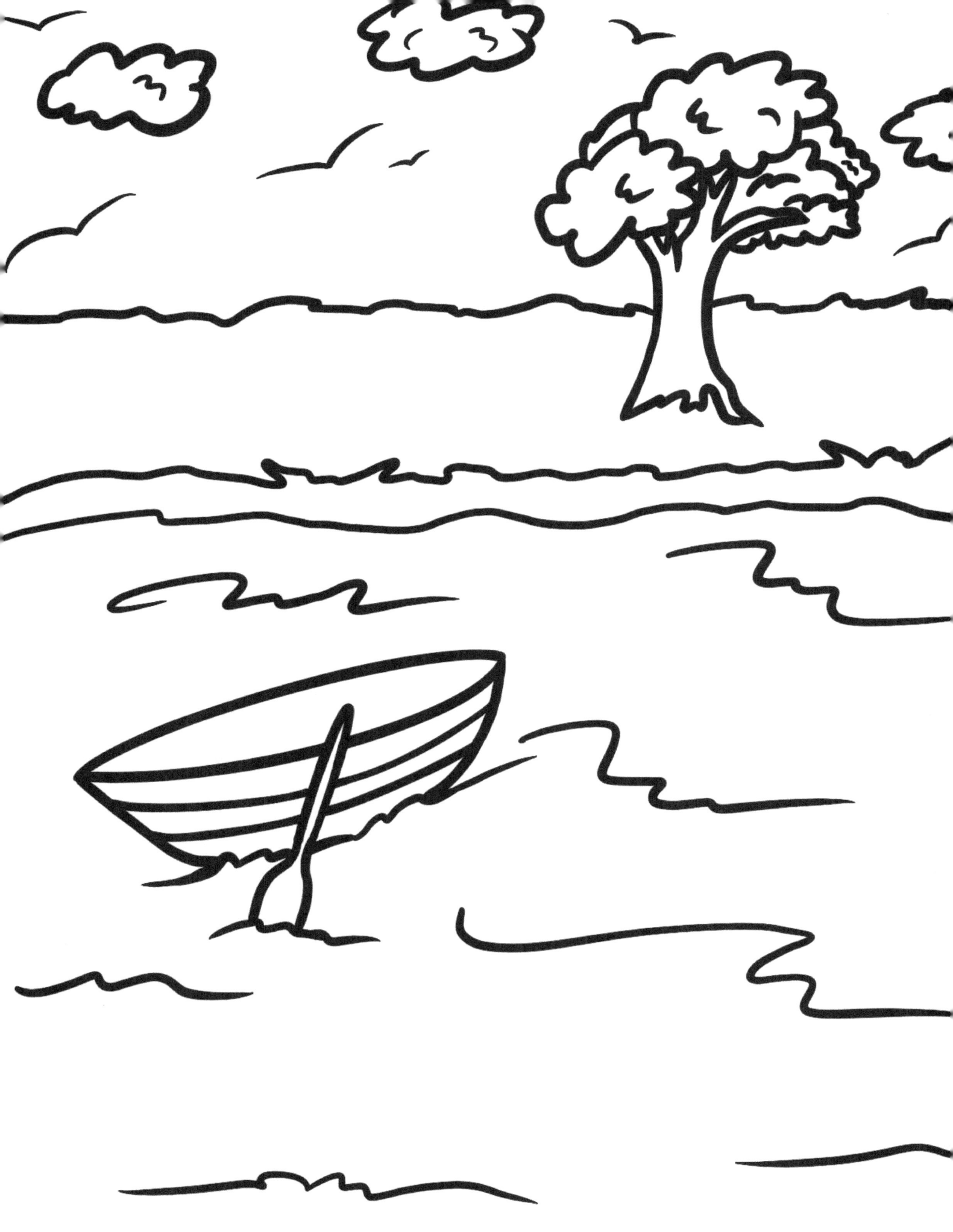

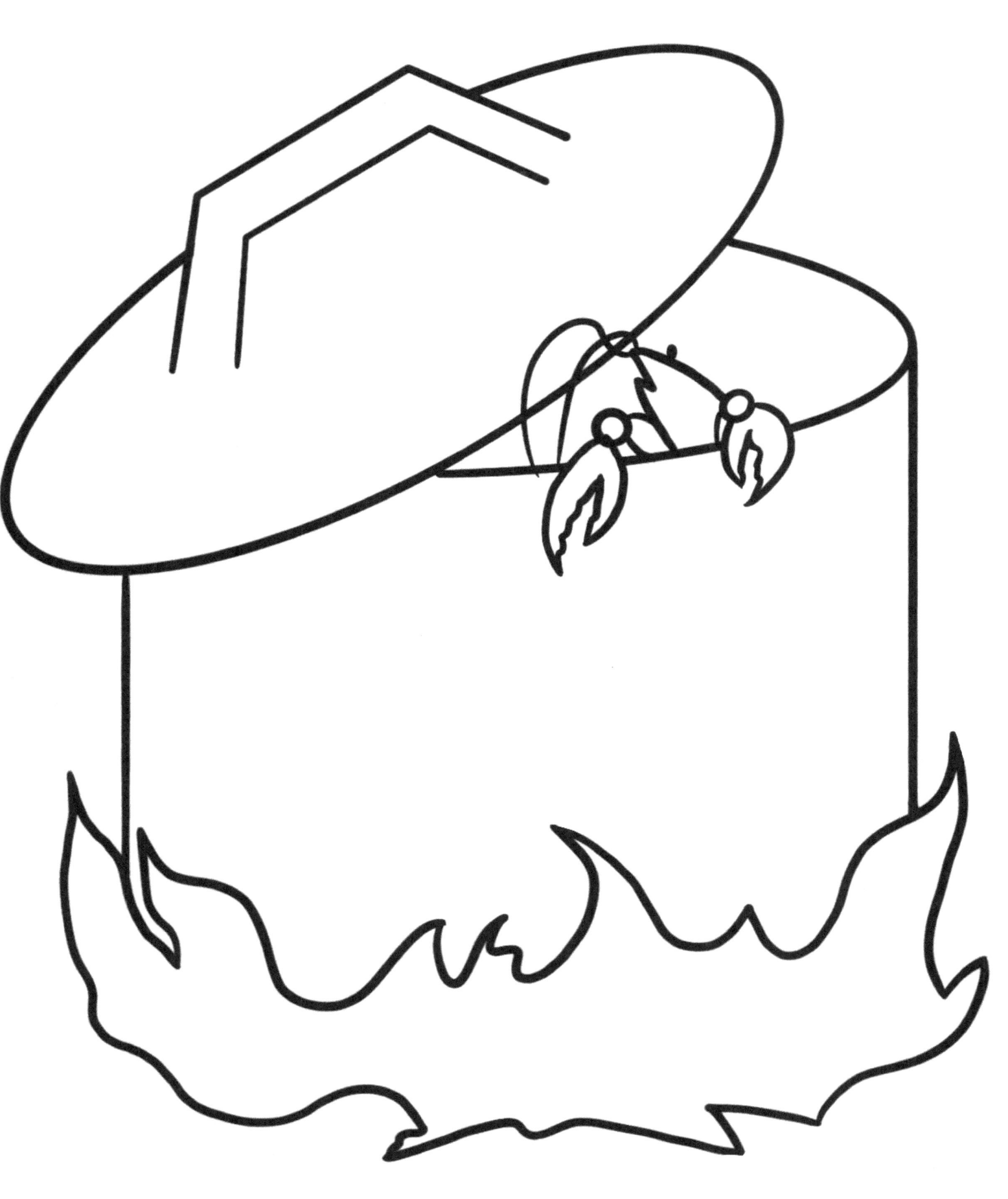

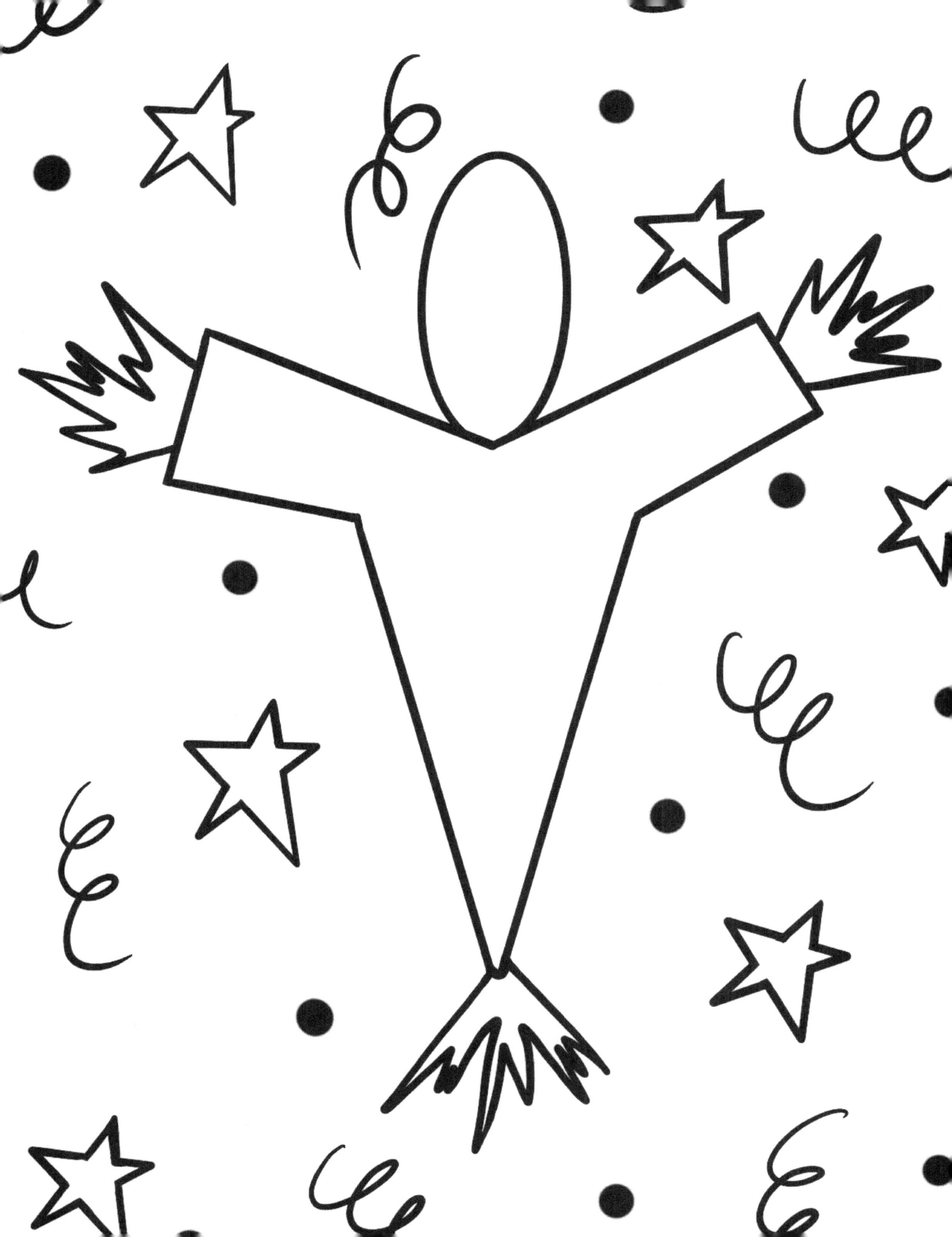

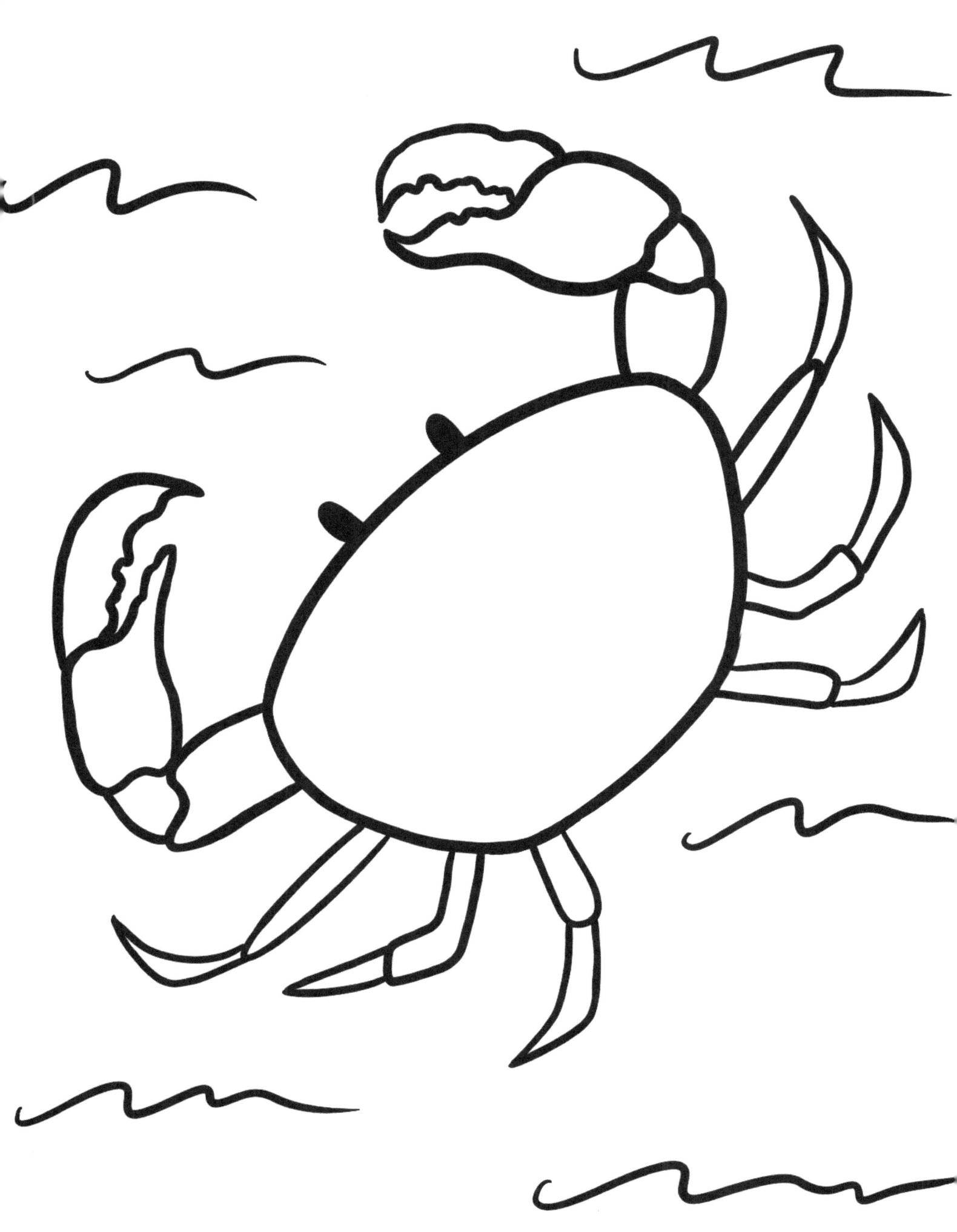

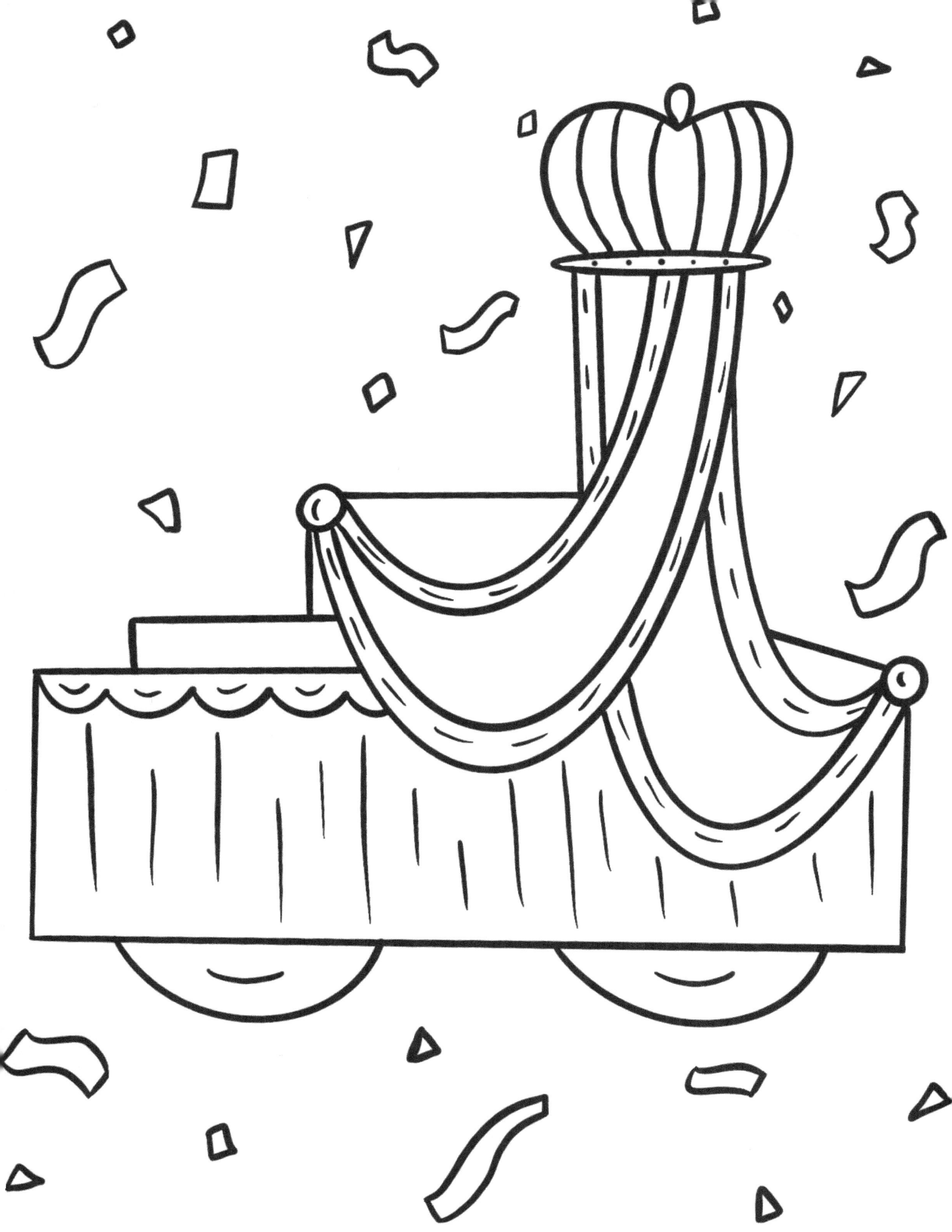

www.ingramcontent.com/pod-product-compliance
Lightning Source LLC
Chambersburg PA
CBHW080941220526
45465CB00008BA/3114